LETTERS OF NOTE: WAR

Letters of Note was born in 2009 with the launch
of lettersofnote.com, a website celebrating
old-fashioned correspondence that has since
been visited over 100 million times. The first
Letters of Note volume was published in October
2013, followed later that year by the first
Letters Live, an event at which world-class
performers delivered remarkable letters
to a live audience.

Since then, these two siblings have grown side
by side, with *Letters of Note* becoming an
international phenomenon, and Letters
Live shows being staged at iconic venues
around the world, from London's Royal Albert Hall
to the theatre at the Ace Hotel in Los Angeles.

You can find out more at lettersofnote.com and
letterslive.com. And now you can also listen to the
audio editions of the new series of *Letters of Note*,
read by an extraordinary cast drawn from the
wealth of talent that regularly takes part in
the acclaimed Letters Live shows.

Letters of Note

WAR

COMPILED BY

Shaun Usher

PENGUIN BOOKS

For Peace

PENGUIN BOOKS
An imprint of Penguin Random House LLC
penguinrandomhouse.com

First published in Great Britain by Canongate Books Ltd 2020
Published in Penguin Books 2020

Compilation and introductions copyright © 2020 by Shaun Usher
Penguin supports copyright. Copyright fuels creativity, encourages
diverse voices, promotes free speech, and creates a vibrant culture.
Thank you for buying an authorized edition of this book and for
complying with copyright laws by not reproducing, scanning,
or distributing any part of it in any form without permission.
You are supporting writers and allowing Penguin to
continue to publish books for every reader.

Page 131 constitutes an extension of this copyright page.

Library of Congress Control Number: 2020940143
ISBN 9780143134640 (paperback)
ISBN 9780525506454 (ebook)

Printed in the United States of America
1 3 5 7 9 10 8 6 4 2

Set in Joanna MT

CONTENTS

INTRODUCTION ix

01 THERE'S NO HOPE IN WAR
Kurt Vonnegut to the Draft Board 2

02 I SHALL DIE WITH MY HEAD HELD HIGH
Blanca Brissac Vázquez to her son, Enrique 5

03 THE HISTORY OF A BATTLE
Duke of Wellington to John Wilson Croker 8

04 ALL THESE MUST BE FREE
Rabbi Morris Frank to his son, Henry 11

05 I WILL DRIVE THEM AWAY
King Béhanzin to Alfred-Amédée Dodds 14

06 FLEETS AND ARMIES WOULD BE HELPLESS
Mark Twain to Nikola Tesla 16

07 MY FELLOW SOLDIERS HAVE NO BEER
First and Second Centuries AD 20

08 HOW IT HURTS TO WRITE THIS
Eleanor Wimbish to her son,
William R. Stocks 22

09 WE ARE YOURS IN THIS SISTERHOOD OF SORROW
The women of England and the women of Germany and Austria 28

10 HAIL EUROPE!
Gajan Singh to Sirdar Harbans Singh 34

11 THIS RAIN OF ATOMIC BOMBS WILL INCREASE MANYFOLD IN FURY
Luis Alvarez to Ryōkichi Sagane 37

12 YOU BABYLONIAN SCULLION
Mehmed IV and the Zaporozhian Cossacks 40

13 MUST WE HATE THEM?
Canute Frankson to a friend 44

14 WAR IS CRUELTY, AND YOU CANNOT REFINE IT
James M. Calhoun, E.E. Rawson and S.C. Wells and William T. Sherman 50

15 THE GOD OF BATTLES
Lord Horatio Nelson to Lady Emma Hamilton 60

16 EXHAUSTED BUT EXHILARATED
June Wandrey to her sister, Betty 64

17 KEEP IT AND HONOR IT ALWAYS
Tom O'Sullivan to his son, Conor 70

18 PLEASE SPARE HER
Poppy, Lionel and Freda Hewlett and Lord Kitchener 73

19 THE MOST EXTRAORDINARY SCENE
Captain Reginald John Armes to his wife 76

20 CORNWALLIS AND HIS ARMY ARE OURS
Alexander Hamilton to his wife, Elizabeth 83

21 WHY CAN'T WE HAVE A SOLDIER'S PAY?
James Henry Gooding to President Abraham Lincoln   86

22 THIS IS QUITE TRUE
Evelyn Waugh to Laura Waugh   92

23 THE ZULUS WERE ON US AT ONCE
Lieutenant Henry Curling to his mother   96

24 THESE THINGS AREN'T TRIVIAL TO ME
Captain Rodney R. Chastant to his parents   104

25 MY DEAR FAMILY, PLEASE FORGIVE ME
Alaa abd al-Akeedi to his family   108

26 FOR THE SAKE OF HUMANITY
Mohandas Gandhi to Adolf Hitler   110

27 THE SONS OF HAM
M.W. Saddler to the *Freeman* newspaper   117

28 IT IS ALL GOING TO HELL
Martha Gellhorn to Eleanor Roosevelt   122

29 I HAVE DONE MY DUTY
John Duesbery to his mother   126

30 SLEEP WELL MY LOVE
Brian Keith to Dave   128

PERMISSION CREDITS   131

ACKNOWLEDGEMENTS   132

A letter is a time bomb, a message in a bottle, a spell, a cry for help, a story, an expression of concern, a ladle of love, a way to connect through words. This simple and brilliantly democratic art form remains a potent means of communication and, regardless of whatever technological revolution we are in the middle of, the letter lives and, like literature, it always will.

INTRODUCTION

War carries within it the greatest extremes of human nature: in the violence, slaughter and destruction it reveals the worst of us; in the acts of bravery, loyalty and selflessness, it demonstrates the very best. For soldiers, sometimes continents away from home, surrounded by strangers trained – like themselves – explicitly to kill, while finely tuned machines of war thunder overhead, each day, each moment, could very well be their last. For the families, friends and loved ones they leave behind – the very people for whom they are risking their lives – the trepidation lies in the silence and the not knowing.

For both the soldier and those left at home, a letter can act as a bridge. For the soldier, stripped of all that is dear, a letter from home can recall a life of peace, away from the bloodshed, or be an epistolary embrace from a world agonisingly far from physical reach. The simple act of holding an envelope covered in familiar handwriting, or catching sight of a pre-war postal address, can bring warmth and light where there is none. Letters from the frontlines of war potentially bring less comfort, but are a vital sign of life, allowing the miles, countries and continents between correspondents to fall away for a few brief moments.

Put simply, the letter can hold enormous power, and if only for a few minutes each day can offer a necessary distraction from the scenes of distress and carnage regularly faced by servicemen and women, and boost morale at a time when morale is essential for survival.

Which is why, during World War I alone, the British Army postal service moved heaven and earth to deliver two billion letters to and from soldiers on the Western Front, fully aware that the psychological benefits resulting from this form of communication — often their *sole* form of communication — could be the difference between victory and defeat. This is also why, during the American Civil War, Postmaster-General Montgomery Blair made it almost impossible for Confederate troops to correspond with loved ones, by devaluing Confederate stamps and returning to sender all letters headed towards Confederate camps — a cruel but effective tactic that further served to isolate and demoralise the opposition.

But war correspondence has an important purpose other than lifting spirits: to generate documentary evidence of battles otherwise unreported, and thus leave for future generations first-hand accounts of wars that changed history and quite possibly affected their lives, and the lives of their ancestors, in myriad ways. Thanks to the many archives and museums around the world that work to preserve these documents, historians are able to trace our past and fill in the blanks so often left by destructive wars. Without these letters, our understanding of our ancestors and ourselves would be greatly reduced.

Letters of Note: War is a collection of these moments: a celebration of correspondence that has narrated the battles that have shaped our world, from the first century AD to the modern day. On your journey through the battlefields and home fronts described here, you will read letters from army generals, letters from the frontlines, letters from military nurses, letters from loved ones, letters from journalists. You will read a dying soldier's last letter to his mother; a letter dropped from a bomber above Japan minutes before the atomic bomb flattened Nagasaki; a heartening exchange between the young owner of a pony and the Secretary of State for War; and you will realise that nothing much has changed as you read some surprisingly everyday letters from Roman Britain. No emotion remains unexpressed.

These war letters barely scratch the surface of the billions that are out there, the vast majority of which will never see the light of day as they sit in attics across the globe gathering dust. The next time you're up there, take them out of that box and let them breathe. They probably have a story to tell you.

Shaun Usher
2020

The Letters

LETTER 01
THERE'S NO HOPE IN WAR
Kurt Vonnegut to the Draft Board
28 November 1967

For as long as there have been wars, there have been conscientious objectors – people who refuse to fight in the military on principle – and the earliest on record dates back to the year 295, when Maximilian of Tebessa declined to enlist in the Roman Army. He was swiftly beheaded. Between the years 1965 and 1970, approximately 160,000 people attempted to abstain from military service in relation to the Vietnam War, including, in 1967, Mark Vonnegut, son of celebrated novelist Kurt Vonnegut. As Mark attempted to remove himself from proceedings through the standard channels, his father decided to strengthen Mark's chances by writing to the Draft Board.

THE LETTER

November 28, 1967

To Draft Board #1,
Selective Service,
Hyannis, Mass.

Gentlemen:
My son Mark Vonnegut is registered with you. He is now in the process of requesting classification as a conscientious objector. I thoroughly approve of what he is doing. It is in keeping with the way I have raised him. All his life he has learned hatred for killing from me.

I was a volunteer in the Second World War. I was an infantry scout, saw plenty of action, was finally captured and served about six months as a prisoner of war in Germany. I have a Purple Heart. I was honorably discharged. I am entitled, it seems to me, to pass on to my son my opinion of killing. I don't even hunt or fish any more. I have some guns which I inherited, but they are covered with rust.

This attitude toward killing is a matter between my God and me. I do not participate much in organized religion. I have read the Bible a lot. I preach, after a fashion. I write books which express my disgust for people who find it easy and reasonable to kill.

We say grace at meals, taking turns. Every member of my family has been called upon often to thank God for blessings which have been ours. What Mark is doing now is in the service of God, Whose Son was exceedingly un-warlike.

There isn't a grain of cowardice in this. Mark is a strong, courageous young man. What he is doing requires more guts than I ever had—and more decency.

My family has been in this country for five generations now. My ancestors came here to escape the militaristic madness and tyranny of Europe, and to gain the freedom to answer the dictates of their own consciences. They and their descendents have been good citizens and proud to be Americans. Mark is proud to be an American, and, in his father's opinion, he is being an absolutely first-rate citizen now.

He will not hate.

He will not kill.

There's no hope in that. There's no hope in war.

Yours truly,

Kurt Vonnegut, Jr.

LETTER 02
I SHALL DIE WITH MY HEAD HELD HIGH
Blanca Brissac Vázquez to her son, Enrique
5 August 1939

Beginning in July 1936, the Spanish Civil War lasted for two years and eight months and resulted in hundreds of thousands of deaths; the dissolution of the country's democratic government, the Second Spanish Republic; and, in its place, the installation of a military dictatorship headed by Francisco Franco that lasted until his death in 1975. Executions were commonplace during the initial conflict, and they continued for some time afterwards, too, as Franco's forces exerted their authority and removed potential troublemakers. It was during this period of cleansing, weeks after the war ended, that thirteen young women later known as las Trece Rosas (the Thirteen Roses) – most of whom were members of the Unified Socialist Youth – were arrested and sentenced to death. They were executed by firing squad on the morning of 5 August 1939. Hours before they took their last breath, one of the Roses, twenty-nine-year-old Blanca Brissac Vázquez, wrote to her son.

THE LETTER

My dear, my precious son,
I'm thinking of you in my last moments. I only think of my darling boy, who is now a young man, and knows to be as honourable as his parents were. Forgive me, my son, if I ever did wrong by you. Forget that, son, do not remember me like that, as you know how distressed it makes me.

I will die with my head held high. Just be good: you know that better than anyone, dear Quique.

All I ask of you is to be good, very good, always. Love everybody and do not hold grudges against those who sentenced your parents to death, not ever. Good people never hold grudges and you must be a good, hardworking man. Follow the example of your Papa. Won't you promise me that, my dear son, in my last moments? Stay with my beloved Cuca and always be a son to her and my sisters. Take care of them when they grow old. Make it your duty when you become a man. I won't say any more. Your father and I face death defiantly. If your father has confessed and taken communion, I am not aware, as I won't see him again until I face the firing squad. I myself have confessed.

Enrique, never forget the memory of your

parents. Go to communion, well prepared, with a proper foundation of religion, as I was taught to do. I would keep writing to you to the very last moment, but I must say goodbye. My dearest son, until we meet again. My love for all eternity.

Blanca

LETTER 03
THE HISTORY OF A BATTLE
Duke of Wellington to John Wilson Croker
8 August 1815

On 18 June 1815, in Braine-l'Alleud, Belgium, the British and Prussian armies joined forces to defeat the French in the Battle of Waterloo, the last conflict of the twelve-year-long Napoleonic Wars. In August, two months after commanding the British to victory, the Duke of Wellington was contacted by the First Secretary to the Admiralty, John Wilson Croker, who, as both a statesman and an author, was keen to see published a detailed written account of this most historic of wars. It seems only right, then, that he should have written to the person at the very top of the tree – someone who witnessed more of the conflict than most – for his opinion on such an endeavour. This was the Duke of Wellington's reply.

THE LETTER

Paris, 8th August, 1815

My Dear Sir,

I have received your letter of the 2nd, regarding the battle of Waterloo. The object which you propose to yourself is very difficult of attainment, and if really attained is not a little invidious. The history of a battle is not unlike the history of a ball. Some individuals may recollect all the little events of which the great result is the battle won or lost; but no individual can recollect the order in which, or the exact moment at which, they occurred, which makes all the difference as to their value or importance.

Then the faults or the misbehaviour of some gave occasion for the distinction of others, and perhaps were the cause of material losses; and you cannot write a true history of a battle without including the faults and misbehaviour of part at least of those engaged.

Believe me that every man you see in a military uniform is not a hero; and that, although in the account given of a general action, such as that of Waterloo, many instances of individual heroism must be passed over unrelated, it is better for the general interests to leave those parts of the story untold, than to tell the whole truth.

If, however, you should still think it right to turn your attention to this subject, I am most ready to give you every assistance and information in my power.

Believe me, &c.
WELLINGTON

LETTER 04
ALL THESE MUST BE FREE
Rabbi Morris Frank to his son, Henry
1 May 1944

Approximately 1.5 million Jews enlisted with the Allied forces during World War II in an effort to defeat the armies of Nazi Germany, Japan and Italy, and as a result, close to 300 rabbis also signed up to work as Jewish chaplains wherever such support may have been needed, be it on the frontline or in concentration camps. One of the first to set foot on German soil and hold a service for the troops was Rabbi Morris Frank of the Fourth Infantry Division, who was born in Chattanooga, Tennessee, in 1906 and ordained in 1935 by the Jewish Theological Seminary of America. Frank worked tirelessly to connect with and offer comfort not just to his division's Jewish contingent, but to people of all faiths, and his efforts were widely appreciated. In May 1944, weeks before the Normandy Landings took place and with family on his mind, Frank took a moment to write one of many letters home – this one to his young son, Henry.

THE LETTER

1 May '44

Dear Son-

A few days ago I paid another visit to the school for refugee children. You remember — I wrote you about the school where young boys and girls were brot over from parts of Europe. These children had no homes — and nothing to eat. The cruel Nazis had bombed their cities — and they were left without any place to go. I know you would want to help these children so I went to see them and brot them some fruit juices, candy, cookies, and chewing gum. This made them very happy. Seeing them happy made me think of you. Thank God, Henry, you live in America. You can show your thankfulness by helping America stay free — by seeing that everyone has freedom. After this war — and when you grow up — there will be plenty to do and you must learn to do it. It will be your job to help people all over the world keep peace. It will be up to you to do your part to do away with war. Henry — you must always remember that every child whether he is the son of a Hindu, or a little Chinese boy, or a child of a Ukraine peasant, whether he is a youngster born in Burma, or he is one of our sharecropper's children or whether he is a Jewish child in one of Europe's Ghettos — all these must be free — and they must have food. They must be free to think, to say, and to [do] what they think is right. It's a big job, Son, but I know you can be of help — and I want you to be useful.

Henry you can't imagine how happy and thrilled I was to learn of your visit to Grandma and Grandpa in Chattanooga. You certainly made their Passover happy. I think your Mamma is just too precious—

Which reminds me, Son. Have you been taking good care of your Mother? You know we both think she is wonderful — the best Mamma in the whole world — and just now with me away — its up to you to take care of her. See that she is happy — and not lonesome. Once in awhile tell her you love her — and tell her that your Daddy loves her very much.

I am sending you a few pictures. They are for my only Son from his only Daddy.

Give Mamma a big hug and a big kiss for me. Give your Grandma a kiss for me — And to you I send all my love —

Your Daddy

Morris

LETTER 05
I WILL DRIVE THEM AWAY
King Béhanzin to Alfred-Amédée Dodds
1892

In 1889, Béhanzin succeeded his father to become ruler of the Kingdom of Dahomey, a West African region famous for its Dahomey Amazons, a widely feared 5,000-strong regiment of female warriors that formed in the late 1600s. The Amazons remained in existence through to the Second Franco-Dahomean War, the 1892–94 conflict which ultimately saw Béhanzin surrender and Dahomey become a French colony, and the Amazons were disbanded under French rule. Problems first arose in 1890, when Béhanzin refused to honour a treaty signed years before by his father; two years later, with tensions reaching boiling point, he received a note from the commander of the French forces, Alfred-Amédée Dodds, demanding he surrender. This letter was Béhanzin's defiant reply. Dodds soon declared war, and the Amazons were no match for the French forces.

THE LETTER

France wishes war. Let her know that I am stronger and more determined than my father. I have never done anything to France that she should make war on me. I have never gone to France either to take the wives or daughters of the French. If they wish to take the seacoast, I will cut down all the palm trees. I will poison them. If they have not what to eat, let them go elsewhere. Every other nation, German, English, Portuguese, can come into my kingdom. But the French, I will drive them away. I am the friend of the whites; ready to receive them when they wish to come to see me, but prompt to make war whenever they wish.

LETTER 06
FLEETS AND ARMIES WOULD BE HELPLESS
Mark Twain to Nikola Tesla
1898

In April 1898, following the sinking of USS Midway *in Havana Harbour, the US intervened in Cuba's fight for independence against the Spanish, thus beginning the Spanish–American War, a four-month battle that resulted in more than 1,000 casualties. It was against this backdrop, in May, that Madison Square Garden in New York hosted the Electrical Exhibition, an event which saw the industry's leading lights proudly display their latest inventions. One such inventor was the 'Father of Electricity', Nikola Tesla, who perplexed the assembled audience by unveiling a four-foot-long boat that travelled around an indoor pond, seemingly steering itself but captained, in fact, by Tesla from some distance. News of his ground-breaking, radio-controlled vehicle spread quickly, with many imagining its military applications, and later that year, Tesla showed the technology to a stunned journalist from the* New York Herald, *who ran a piece headlined: TESLA DECLARES HE WILL ABOLISH WAR. Worldwide patents followed, as did a letter from Vienna offering business assistance, written by Tesla's friend, Mark Twain.*

THE LETTER

HOTEL KRANTZ
Wein/I.Neuer Markt 6
Nov. 17
1898

Dear Mr. Tesla —
Have you Austrian and English patents on that destructive terror which you have been inventing?—& if so, won't you set a price upon them & concession me to sell them? I know cabinet ministers of both countries—& of Germany, too; likewise William II.

I shall be in Europe a year, yet.

Here in the hotel the other night when some interested men were discussing means to persuade the nations to join with the Czar & disarm, I advised them to seek something more sure than disarmament by perishable paper-contract — invite the great inventors to contrive something against which fleets & armies would be helpless, & thus make war thenceforth impossible. I did not suspect that you were already attending to that, & getting ready to introduce into the earth permanent peace & disarmament in a practical & mandatory way.

I know you are a very busy man, but will you steal time to drop me a line?

Sincerely Yours,

Mark Twain

'I DID NOT SUSPECT THAT YOU WERE ALREADY ATTENDING TO THAT, & GETTING READY TO INTRODUCE INTO THE EARTH PERMANENT PEACE & DISARMAMENT IN A PRACTICAL & MANDATORY WAY.'
— Mark Twain

LETTER 07
MY FELLOW SOLDIERS HAVE NO BEER
First and Second Centuries AD

In 1973 archaeologists working near Hadrian's Wall in England, the northern border of the Roman Empire, unearthed the first batch of what are now known as the Vindolanda tablets: hundreds of thin slivers of wood upon which brief but invaluably insightful letters had been written towards the end of the first century AD, penned in ink in Old Roman Cursive. To this day, letters are still being discovered at the Roman fort of Vindolanda, many of which relate to the life of the soldiers who once fought there during a time of unrest; snapshots of military life 2,000 long years ago when, actually, things seem quite familiar.

THE LETTERS

The Britons are unprotected by armour. There are very many cavalry. The cavalry do not use swords, nor do the pathetic Brits mount in order to throw javelins.

* * *

I have sent you ... pairs of socks from Sattua, two pairs of sandals and two pairs of underpants, two pairs of sandals ... Greet ...ndes, Elpis, Iu..., ...enus, Tetricus and all your messmates with whom I pray that you live in the greatest good fortune.

* * *

Masculus to Cerialis his king, greetings. Please, my lord, give instructions on what you want us to do tomorrow. Are we all to return with the standard, or just half of us? ... most fortunate and be well-disposed towards me. My fellow soldiers have no beer. Please order some to be sent.

LETTER 08
HOW IT HURTS TO WRITE THIS
Eleanor Wimbish to her son, William R. Stocks
13 February 1984

US Army Sergeant William Reed Stocks was killed in 1969 when the helicopter in which he was travelling crashed in Vietnam. He was twenty-one years old. At the Vietnam Veterans Memorial in Washington, D.C., his name can be found engraved in the granite of panel number thirty-two, a permanent reminder of his service and the life he lost so early. For many years after his death, at the same panel, one could also find many unmailed letters addressed to Billy, written by his mother throughout the year and placed beneath his name. This is just one.

THE LETTER

Dear Bill,

Today is February 13, 1984. I came to this black wall again to see and touch your name and as I do I wonder if anyone ever stops to realize that next to your name, on this black wall, is your mother's heart. A heart broken 15 years ago today, when you lost your life in Vietnam.

And as I look at your name, William R. Stocks, I think of how many, many times I used to wonder how scared and homesick you must have been in that strange country called Vietnam. And if and how it might have changed you, for you were the most happy-go-lucky kid in the world, hardly ever sad or unhappy. And until the day I die I will see you as you laughed at me, even when I was very mad at you, and the next thing I knew, we were laughing together.

But on this past New Year's Day I had my answer, I talked by phone to a friend of yours, from Michigan, who spent your last Christmas and the last four months of your life with you. Jim told me how you died, for he was there and saw the helicopter crash. He told me how you had flown your quota and had not been scheduled to fly that day. How the regular pilot was unable to fly that day and had been replaced by someone with less experience. How they did not know the exact cause of the crash. How it was either hit by enemy fire or they hit a pole or something unknown. How the blades went through the chopper and hit you. How you lived about a half-hour, but were unconscious and therefore did not suffer.

He said that your jobs were like sitting ducks. They would send you men out to draw the enemy into the open and that they would send in the big guns and planes to take over. Meantime, death came to so many of you.

He told me how, after a while over there, instead of a yellow streak, the men got a mean streak down their backs. Each day the streak got bigger and the men became meaner. Everyone but you, Bill. He said how you stayed the same, happy-go-lucky guy that you were when you arrived in Vietnam. How your warmth and friendliness drew the guys to you. How your [lieutenant] gave you the nickname of Spanky, and soon your group, Jim included, were all known as Spanky's gang. How when you died it made it so much harder on them for you were their moral support. And he said how you, of all people, should never have been the one to die.

Oh, God, how it hurts to write this. But I must

face it and then put it to rest. I know that after Jim talked to me, he must have re-lived it all over again and suffered so. Before I hung up the phone I told Jim I loved him. Loved him for just being your close friend and for sharing the last days of your life with you and for being there with you when you died. How lucky you were to have him for a friend, and how lucky he was to have had you.

Later that same day I received a phone call from a mother in Billings, Montana. She had lost her daughter, her only child, a year ago. She needed someone to talk to for no one would let her talk about the tragedy. She said she had seen me on CNN-TV on New Year's Eve, after the Christmas letter I wrote to you and left at this Memorial had drawn newspaper and television attention. She said she had been thinking about me all day and just had to talk to me. She talked to me of her pain, and seemingly needed me to help her with it. I cried for this heartbroken mother, and after I hung up the phone I laid my head down and cried so hard for her. Here was a mother calling me for help with her pain over the loss of her child, a grown daughter. And as I sobbed I thought, how can I help her with her pain when I have never completely been able to cope with my own?

They tell me the letters I write to you and leave

here at this memorial are waking others up to the fact that there is still much pain left, after all these years, from the Vietnam War.

But this I know: I would rather to have had you for 21 years, and all the pain that goes with losing you, than never to have had you at all.

Mom

> 'AS I SOBBED I THOUGHT, HOW CAN I HELP HER WITH HER PAIN WHEN I HAVE NEVER COMPLETELY BEEN ABLE TO COPE WITH MY OWN?'
> — *Eleanor Wimbish*

LETTER 09
WE ARE YOURS IN THIS SISTERHOOD OF SORROW
The women of England and the women of Germany and Austria
Christmas 1914

Born in Cornwall in 1860, activist Emily Hobhouse first came to prominence at the turn of the twentieth century when, having travelled to South Africa as the Second Boer War raged, she alerted the British public to the plight of the many women and children who were being held there in concentration camps. Her courageous campaigning and fundraising on this front were tireless. Years later, when World War I began, she was similarly active and, as 1914 drew to a close, in an effort to promote peace, Hobhouse wrote this open letter to the women of Germany and Austria and amassed signatures from 100 other British suffragists. It was printed in the pages of a magazine, Jus Suffragii, *published by the International Women's Suffrage Alliance. Three months later, a reply appeared, also published in the same magazine, signed by 155 feminists from Germany and Austria.*

THE LETTERS

TO THE WOMEN OF GERMANY & AUSTRIA

Sisters,

Some of us wish to send you a word at this sad Christmastide though we can but speak through the Press. The Christmas message sounds like mockery to a world at war, but those of us who wished and still wish for peace may surely offer a solemn greeting to such of you who feel as we do. Do not let us forget that our very anguish unites us, that we are passing together through the same experiences of pain and grief.

Caught in the grip of terrible Circumstance, what can we do? Tossed on this turbulent sea of human conflict, we can but moor ourselves to those calm shores whereon stand, like rocks, the eternal verities — Love, Peace, Brotherhood.

We pray you to believe that come what may we hold to our faith in Peace and Goodwill between nations; while technically at enmity in obedience to our rulers, we own allegiance to that higher law which bids us live at peace with all men.

Though our sons are sent to slay each other, and our hearts are torn by the cruelty of this fate, yet through pain supreme we will be true to our common womanhood. We will let no bitterness enter in this tragedy, made sacred by the life-blood of our best, nor mar with hate the heroism of their sacrifice. Though much has been done on all sides you will, as deeply as ourselves, deplore, shall we not steadily refuse to give credence to those false tales so freely told us, each of the other?

We hope it may lessen your anxiety to learn we are doing our utmost to soften the lot of your civilians and war prisoners within our shores, even as we rely on your goodness of heart to do the same for ours in Germany and Austria.

Do you not feel with us that the vast slaughter in our opposing armies is a stain on civilization and Christianity, and that still deeper horror is aroused at the thought of those innocent victims, the countless women, children, babes, old and sick, pursued by famine, disease and death in the devastated areas, both East and West?

As we saw in South Africa and the Balkan States, the brunt of modern war falls upon non-combatants, and the conscience of the world cannot bear the sight.

Is it not our mission to preserve life? Do not humanity and commonsense alike prompt us to join hands with the women of neutral countries, and urge our rulers to stay further bloodshed?

Relief, however colossal, can reach but few. Can we sit still and let the helpless die in their thousands, as die they must — unless we rouse ourselves in the name of Humanity to save them? There is but one way to do this. We must all urge that peace be made with appeal to Wisdom and Reason. Since in the last resort it is these which must decide the issues, can they begin too soon, if it is to save the womanhood and childhood as well as the manhood of Europe?

Even through the clash of arms we treasure our poet's vision, and already seem to hear

'A hundred nations swear that there shall be
Pity and Peace and Love among the good and free.'

May Christmas hasten that day. Peace on Earth is gone, but by renewal of our faith that it still reigns at the heart of things, Christmas should strengthen both you and us and all womanhood to strive for its return.

We are yours in this sisterhood of sorrow.
[Signed by Emily Hobhouse and 100 others]

* * *

OPEN LETTER IN REPLY TO THE OPEN CHRISTMAS LETTER FROM ENGLISHWOMEN TO GERMAN AND AUSTRIAN WOMEN

To our English sisters, sisters of the same race, we express in the name of many German women our warm and heartfelt thanks for their Christmas greetings, which we only heard of lately.

This message was a confirmation of what we foresaw — namely, that women of the belligerent countries, with all faithfulness, devotion, and love to their country, can go beyond it and maintain true solidarity with the women of other belligerent nations, and that really civilised women never lose their humanity.

If English women alleviated misery and distress at this time, relieved anxiety, and gave help irrespective of nationality, let them accept the warmest thanks of German women and the true assurance that they are and were prepared to do likewise. In war time we are united by the same unspeakable suffering of all nations taking part in the war. Women of all nations have the same love of justice, civilisation, and beauty, which are all destroyed by war. Women of all nations have the same hatred for barbarity, cruelty, and destruction, which accompany every war.

Women, creators and guardians of life, must loathe war, which destroys life. Through the smoke of battle and thunder of cannon of hostile peoples, through death, terror, destruction, and unending pain and anxiety, there glows like the dawn of a coming better day the deep community of feeling of many women of all nations.

May this feeling lay the immovable foundation for the building up of German, English, and international relations, which must finally lead to a strong international law of the peoples, so that the peoples of Europe may never again be visited with such wars as these.

Warm sisterly greetings to Englishwomen who share these feelings!

LETTER 10
HAIL EUROPE!
Gajan Singh to Sirdar Harbans Singh
25 July 1916

A few months into World War I, at the peak of enlistment, the British Indian Army boasted 548,311 soldiers who were ready to risk their lives fighting for the British Empire; by the time the war had ended four years later, more than a million had done precisely that, voluntarily, with close to 75,000 losing their lives in the process. It is no exaggeration to say that without them, the outcome of the Great War would have looked very different. In Europe alone, letters sent by Indian soldiers totalled upwards of 10,000 each week, of which this is just one. While stationed in France on 25 July 1916, one sepoy, a Sikh with the 18th Lancers named Gajan Singh, described the current scene in a letter home that was originally written in Urdu.

THE LETTER

> 25th July 1916
> 18th Lancers
> France

At the present time the war has reached a degree of violence which it is impossible to conceive. The number of thousands of shots per second fired by the artillery cannot be counted, and as regards rifle fire it would be quite impossible to estimate the intensity of it. When it rains there are a few spots here and there, perhaps, which the moisture fails to touch, but not even the smallest portion of the surface of the ground has escaped damage by rifle, bomb and shell-fire. If you were to estimate five shots on every square inch of ground you would not be far off the mark. The enemy is now giving ground. His losses have been enormous. The fire of the machine guns and artillery is so rapid that one cannot keep time with it even by chattering one's teeth.

The work of our brave men is worthy to be seen. One forgets the achievements of Bonaparte when one sees what our men have done. How our heroes have gone forward, quite regardless of life, and crushed the head of the enemy on the ground!

Battalion after battalion follow their music, filled with enthusiasm, just as a snake dances to the pipe of the charmer and darts forward to strike. Such intoxicating music has never been played before. Battalions go forward with even step, steadily and firmly, just as an elephant moves along the road swaying slightly from side to side, to show the worth of their valour. Truly even from the enemy's lips they must have wrung applause. Thousands of heroes have arisen in this war as brave and illustrious as was Bonaparte. Even the heavens do not cease from shedding tears on our warriors, so great is their valour. Hail Europe! From time immemorial the fame of your valour has been spread over the whole world!

What in truth can I write and tell you about this war. Things are being done here which stagger the onlooking world. Alas the regulations prevent me from writing more fully, otherwise I would write you a volume of details, the perusal of which would inflame your soul.

LETTER 11
THIS RAIN OF ATOMIC BOMBS WILL INCREASE MANYFOLD IN FURY
Luis Alvarez to Ryōkichi Sagane
August 9 1945

At 11 a.m. on 9 August 1945, just a minute before the second atomic bomb in the space of three days was dropped on Japan, a B-29 bomber named The Great Artiste *quietly dropped three canisters from the sky. Inside each of the canisters, alongside a shockwave gauge designed by American physicist Luis Alvarez, was an unsigned copy of the following letter. Written by Alvarez and two fellow scientists, the letter was addressed to Japanese nuclear physicist Ryōkichi Sagane, a man with whom Alvarez had previously worked at Berkeley, and in it, Alvarez pleaded with him to inform his 'leaders' of the impending 'total annihilation' of their cities. The letter reached Sagane a month later after being found 50km from the centre of devastation, Nagasaki. Alvarez and Sagane finally met again four years later, at which point the letter was finally signed.*

THE LETTER

Headquarters
Atomic Bomb Command
August 9, 1945

To: Prof. R. Sagane
From: Three of your former scientific colleagues during your stay in the United States.

We are sending this as a personal message to urge that you use your influence as a reputable nuclear physicist, to convince the Japanese General Staff of the terrible consequences which will be suffered by your people if you continue in this war.

You have known for several years that an atomic bomb could be built if a nation were willing to pay the enormous cost of preparing the necessary material. Now that you have seen that we have constructed the production plants, there can be no doubt in your mind that all the output of these factories, working 24 hours a day, will be exploded on your homeland.

Within the space of three weeks, we have prooffired one bomb in the American desert, exploded one in Hiroshima, and fired the third this morning.

We implore you to confirm these facts to your leaders, and to do your utmost to stop the destruction and waste of life which can only result in the total annihilation of all your cities, if continued. As scientists, we deplore the use to which a beautiful discovery has been put, but we can assure you that unless Japan surrenders at once, this rain of atomic bombs will increase manyfold in fury.

To my friend Sagane
With best regards from
Louis W. Alvarez

Finally signed
Dec 22, 1949

LETTER 12
YOU BABYLONIAN SCULLION
Mehmed IV and the Zaporozhian Cossacks
c. 1675

In 1675, the Zaporozhian Cossacks – a fierce army of warriors based in what were known as the Wild Fields of Ukraine – whose Koshovyi (chief) at the time was Ivan Sirko, received by courier a letter from Mehmed IV, the Sultan of the Ottoman Empire, in which he rather grandiosely demanded that they cease all aggression and submit to him. Relations were historically fraught, but a recent spate of guerrilla warfare involving the two parties, much of it initiated and won by the Cossacks, had pushed the young sultan to breaking point. His last hope was to write a letter. Rather than accept the demands, Sirko responded with a letter of his own, co-written with his men, which in the 1880s was immortalised in the famous painting, Reply of the Zaporozhian Cossacks to Sultan Mehmed IV of the Ottoman Empire, **by renowned Russian artist Ilya Repin.**

THE LETTERS

Sultan Mehmed IV to the Zaporozhian Cossacks
As the Sultan; son of Muhammad; brother of the sun and moon; grandson and viceroy of God; ruler of the kingdoms of Macedonia, Babylon, Jerusalem, Upper and Lower Egypt; emperor of emperors; sovereign of sovereigns; extraordinary knight, never defeated; steadfast guardian of the tomb of Jesus Christ; trustee chosen by God Himself; the hope and comfort of Muslims; confounder and great defender of Christians – I command you, the Zaporogian Cossacks, to submit to me voluntarily and without any resistance, and to desist from troubling me with your attacks.
  Turkish Sultan Mehmed IV

* * *

Zaporozhian Cossacks to the Turkish Sultan!
O sultan, Turkish devil and damned devil's kith and kin, secretary to Lucifer himself! What the devil kind of knight are you, that can't slay a hedgehog with your naked arse? The devil shits, and your army eats it. You will not, you son of a bitch, make subjects of Christian sons; we've no fear of your army, by land and by sea we will battle with thee, fuck your mother.

You Babylonian scullion, Macedonian wheelwright, brewer of Jerusalem, goat-fucker of Alexandria, swineherd of Greater and Lesser Egypt, pig of Armenia, Podolian thief, catamite of Tartary, hangman of Kamyanets, and fool of all the world and underworld, an idiot before God, grandson of the Serpent, and the crick in our dick. Pig's snout, mare's arse, butcher's dog, unchristened brow, screw your own mother!

So the Zaporozhians declare, you lowlife. You won't even be herding pigs for the Christians. Now we'll conclude, for we don't know the date and don't own a calendar; the moon's in the sky, the year with the Lord, the day's the same over here as it is over there; for this kiss our arse!

Koshovyi otaman Ivan Sirko,
with all the Zaporozhian Host

'WE'VE NO FEAR OF YOUR ARMY, BY LAND AND BY SEA WE WILL BATTLE WITH THEE, FUCK YOUR MOTHER.'

– Memed IV

LETTER 13
MUST WE HATE THEM?
Canute Frankson to a friend
6 July 1937

In April 1937, Jamaican-born mechanic Canute Frankson left his home in Detroit and travelled to Europe to join the Abraham Lincoln Brigade, a group of approximately 2,800 American volunteers who were keen to offer support in the fight against Franco and his army during the Spanish Civil War. Three months after arriving, Frankson wrote a powerful letter to a friend back home in an effort to explain why he, a 'Negro', had chosen to participate in 'a war between whites who for centuries have held us in slavery'. Frankson returned home just over a year later but sadly died shortly afterwards in a road traffic accident. As we know, Franco was ultimately victorious. He ruled Spain until his death in 1975.

THE LETTER

Albacete, Spain
July 6, 1937

My Dear Friend:

I'm sure that by this time you are still waiting for a detailed explanation of what has this international struggle to do with my being here. Since this is a war between whites who for centuries have held us in slavery, and have heaped every kind of insult and abuse upon us, segregated and jim-crowed us; why I, a Negro, who have fought through these years for the rights of my people am here in Spain today.

Because we are no longer an isolated minority group fighting hopelessly against an immense giant, because, my dear, we have joined with, and become an active part of, a great progressive force, on whose shoulders rests the responsibility of saving human civilization from the planned destruction of a small group of degenerates gone mad in their lust for power. Because if we crush Fascism here, we'll save our people in America, and in other parts of the world, from the vicious prosecution, wholesale imprisonment, and slaughter which the Jewish people suffered and are suffering under Hitler's Fascist heels.

All we have to do is to think of the lynching of our people. We can but look back at the pages of American history stained with the blood of Negroes, stink with the burning bodies of our people hanging from trees; bitter with the groans of our tortured loved ones from whose living bodies, ears, fingers, toes, have been cut for souvenirs—living bodies into which red-hot pokers have been thrust. All because of a hate created in the minds of men and women by their masters who keep us all under their heels while they suck our blood, while they live in their bed of ease by exploiting us.

But these people who howl like hungry wolves for our blood, must we hate them? Must we keep the flame which these mastered kindled constantly fed? Are these men and women responsible for the programs of their masters, and the conditions which force them to such degraded depths? I think not. They are tools in the hands of unscrupulous masters. These same people are as hungry as we are. They live in dives and wear rags the same as we do. They too are robbed by the masters, and their faces kept down in the filth of a decayed system. They are our fellowmen. Soon and very soon they and we will understand. Soon many Angelo Herndons will rise from among them, and from among us, and will lead us both against those who live by the stench of our burnt flesh. We will crush them. We will build us a new society—a society of peace and plenty. There will be no color line, no jim-crow trains, no lynching. That is why, my dear, I'm here in Spain.

On the battlefields of Spain we fight for the preservation of democracy. Here, we're laying the foundation for world peace, and for the liberation of my people, and of the human race. Here, where we're engaged in one of the most bitter struggles of human history, there is no color line, no discrimination, no race hatred. There's only one hate, and that is the hate for fascism. We know who our enemies are. The Spanish people are very sympathetic towards us. They are lovely people. I'll tell you about them later.

I promised not to preach, but by all indications this seems more like a sermon than a letter to an old friend. But how can I help it, being face to face with such trying circumstances? I'm quite conscious of the clumsiness of my effort to write you an intimate letter, but your knowledge of my earnestness and sincerity, with your intelligence and patience will enable you to understand and be tolerant. Later, after I've overcome this strain, I'm sure I'll be able to write more intimately. The consciousness of my responsibility for my actions has kept me under terrific strain. Because I think it has caused you a lot of unpleasantness.

Don't think for one moment that the strain of this terrible war or the many miles between us has changed my feelings towards you. Our friendship has meant a great deal to me, and still means much to me. I appreciate it because it has always been a friendship of devoted mutual interest. And I'll do whatever is within my power to maintain it.

No one knows the time he'll die, even under the most favorable conditions. So I, a soldier in active service, must know far less about how far or how close is death. But as long as I hold out I'll keep you in touch with events. Sometimes when I go to the front the shells drop pretty close. Then I think it is only a matter of minutes. After I return here to the base I seem to see life from a new angle. Somehow it seems to be more beautiful. I'd think of you, home and all my friends, then get to working more feverishly than ever. Each of us must give all we have if this Fascist beast is to be destroyed.

After this is over I hope to share my happiness with you. It will be a happiness which could not have been achieved in any other way than having served in a cause so worthy. I hope that the apparent wrong which I committed may be compensated for by the service I'm giving here for the cause of democracy. I hope that you're well, and that you will, or have, forgiven me. My sincere desire is that you are happy, and when this is over that we meet again. But if a Fascist bullet stops me don't worry about it. If I am conscious before I die I don't think I'll be afraid. Of one thing I'm certain: I'll be satisfied that I've done my part.

So long. Until some future date. One never knows when there'll be time to write.

There's so much to do, and so little time in which to do it. Love.

Salude.

Canute

LETTER 14
WAR IS CRUELTY, AND YOU CANNOT REFINE IT
James M. Calhoun, E.E. Rawson and S.C. Wells and William T. Sherman
September 1864

United States Army General William Tecumseh Sherman had one aim in September 1864, and that was to capture, evacuate and then burn to the ground the city of Atlanta, Georgia, thus destroying the Confederate forces' infrastructure, weaponry and will to continue – a tactic of total destruction for which he had become known and feared since being placed in command of the Western armies of the American Civil War by General Ulysses Grant. As his men slowly but steadily approached the city, they received word from its mayor, James M. Calhoun, that certain members of the community were too old or fragile to move on. Sherman's passionate, largely unsympathetic reply made waves, and his troops soon advanced on Atlanta, as promised.

THE LETTERS

ATLANTA, GA.,
September 11, 1864.

Maj. Gen. W.T. SHERMAN:

SIR:
We, the undersigned, mayor and two of the council for the city of Atlanta, for the time being the only legal organ of the people of the said city to express their wants and wishes, ask leave most earnestly, but respectfully, to petition you to reconsider the order requiring them to leave Atlanta. At first view it struck us that the measure would involve extraordinary hardship and loss, but since we have seen the practical execution of it so far as it has progressed, and the individual condition of the people, and heard their statements as to the inconveniences, loss, and suffering attending it, we are satisfied that the amount of it will involve in the aggregate consequences appalling and heart-rending. Many poor women are in advanced state of pregnancy; others now having young children, and whose husbands, for the greater part, are either in the army, prisoners, or dead. Some say, "I have such a

one sick at my house; who will wait on them when I am gone?" Others say, "what are we to do? We have no house to go to, and no means to buy, build, or rent any; no parents, relatives, or friends to go to." Another says, "I will try and take this or that article of property, but such and such things I must leave behind, though I need them much." We reply to them, "General Sherman will carry your property to Rough and Ready, and General Hood will take it thence on," and they will reply to that, "but I want to leave the railroad at such place and cannot get conveyance from there on."

We only refer to a few facts to try to illustrate in part how this measure will operate in practice. As you advanced the people north of this fell back, and before your arrival here a large portion of the people had retired south, so that the country south of this is already crowded and without houses enough to accommodate the people, and we are informed that many are now staying in churches and other outbuildings. This being so, how is it possible for the people still here (mostly women and children) to find any shelter? And how can they live through the winter in the woods? No shelter or subsistence, in the midst of strangers who know them not, and without the power to assist them much, if they were willing to do so. This is but a feeble picture of the consequences of this measure. You know the woe, the horrors and the suffering cannot be described by words; imagination can only conceive of it, and we ask you to take these things into consideration. We know your mind and time are constantly occupied with the duties of your command, which almost deters us from asking your attention to this matter, but thought it might be that you had not considered this subject in all of its awful consequences, and that on more reflection you, we hope, would not make this people an exception to all mankind, for we know of no such instance ever having occurred; surely none such in the United States, and what has this helpless people done, that they should be driven from their homes to wander strangers and outcasts and exiles, and to subsist on charity? We do not know as yet the number of people still here; of those who are here, we are satisfied a respectable number, if allowed to remain at home, could subsist for several months without assistance, and a respectable number for a much longer time, and who might not need assistance at any time. In conclusion, we most earnestly and solemnly petition you to reconsider this order, or modify it, and suffer this unfortunate people to remain at home and enjoy what little means they have.

Respectfully submitted.
JAMES M. CALHOUN,
Mayor.

E.E. RAWSON,
S.C. WELLS,
Councilmen.

* * *

HDQRS. MILITARY DIVISION
OF THE MISSISSIPPI,
In the Field, Atlanta, Ga.,
September 12, 1864.

JAMES M. CALHOUN, Mayor,
E.E. RAWSON, and S.C. WELLS,
Representing City Council of Atlanta:

GENTLEMEN:

I have your letter of the 11th, in the nature of a petition to revoke my orders removing all the inhabitants from Atlanta. I have read it carefully, and give full credit to your statements of the distress that will be occasioned by it, and yet shall not revoke my orders, simply because my orders are not designed to meet the humanities of the case, but to prepare for the future struggles in which millions of good people outside of Atlanta have a deep interest. We must have peace, not only at Atlanta but in all America. To secure this we must stop the war that now desolates our once happy and favored country. To stop war we must defeat the rebel armies that are arrayed against the laws and Constitution, which all must respect and obey. To defeat these armies we must prepare the way to reach them in their recesses provided with the arms and instruments which enable us to accomplish our purpose. Now, I know the vindictive nature of our enemy, and that we may have many years of military operations from this quarter, and therefore deem it wise and prudent to prepare in time. The use of Atlanta for warlike purposes is inconsistent with its character as a home for families. There will be no manufactures, commerce, or agriculture here for the maintenance of families, and sooner or later want will compel the inhabitants to go. Why not go now, when all the arrangements are completed for the transfer, instead of waiting till the plunging shot of contending armies will renew the scenes of the past month? Of course, I do not apprehend any such thing at this moment, but you do not suppose this army will be here until the war is over. I cannot discuss this subject with you fairly, because I cannot impart to you what I propose to do, but I assert that my military plans make it necessary for the inhabitants to go away, and I can only renew my offer of services to make their exodus in any direction as easy and comfortable as possible. You cannot qualify war in harsher terms than I will. War is cruelty and you cannot refine it, and those who brought war into our country deserve all the curses and maledictions a people can pour out. I know I had no hand in making this war, and I know I will make more sacrifices today than any of you to secure peace. But you cannot have peace and a division of our country. If the United States submits to a division now it will not stop, but will go on until we reap the fate of Mexico, which is eternal war. The United States does and must assert its authority wherever it once had power. If it relaxes one bit to pressure it is gone, and I know that such is the national feeling. This feeling assumes various shapes, but always comes back to that of Union. Once admit the Union, once more acknowledge the authority of the National Government, and instead of devoting your houses and streets and roads to the dread uses of war, and this army become at once your protectors and supporters, shielding you from danger, let it come from what quarter it may. I know that a few individuals cannot resist a torrent of error and passion such as swept the South into rebellion, but you can part out so that we may know those who desire a government and those who insist on war and its desolation. You might as well appeal against the thunderstorm as against these terrible hardships of war. They are inevitable, and the only way the people of Atlanta can hope once more to live in peace and quiet at home is to stop the war, which can alone be done by admitting that it began in error and is perpetuated in pride.

We don't want your negroes or your horses or your houses or your lands or anything you have, but we do want, and will have, a just obedience to the laws of the United States. That we will have, and if it involves the destruction of your improvements we cannot help it. You have heretofore read public sentiment in your newspapers that live by falsehood and excitement, and the quicker you seek for truth in other quarters the better for you. I repeat then that by the original compact of government the United States had certain rights in Georgia, which have never been relinquished and never will be; that the South began war by seizing forts, arsenals, mints, customhouses, &c., long before Mr. Lincoln was installed and before the South had one jot or tittle of provocation. I myself have seen in Missouri, Kentucky, Tennessee, and Mississippi hundreds and thousands of women and children fleeing from your armies and desperadoes, hungry and with bleeding feet. In Memphis, Vicksburg, and Mississippi we fed thousands upon thousands of the families of rebel soldiers left on our hands and whom we could not see starve. Now that war comes home to you, you feel very different. You deprecate its horrors, but did not feel them when you sent car-loads of soldiers and ammunition and molded shells and shot to carry war into Kentucky and Tennessee, and desolate the homes of hundreds and thousands of good people who only asked to live in peace at their old homes and under the Government of their inheritance. But these comparisons are idle. I want peace, and believe it can now only be reached through union and war, and I will ever conduct war with a view to perfect an early success. But, my dear sirs, when that peace does come, you may call on me for anything. Then will I share with you the last cracker, and watch with you to shield your homes and families against danger from every quarter. Now you must go, and

take with you the old and feeble, feed and nurse
them and build for them in more quiet places
proper habitations to shield them against the
weather until the mad passions of men cool down
and allow the Union and peace once more to settle
over your old homes at Atlanta.

Yours, in haste,
W.T. SHERMAN,
Major-General, Commanding.

LETTER 15
THE GOD OF BATTLES
Lord Horatio Nelson to Lady Emma Hamilton
19 October 1805

Over the course of five hours on 21 October 1805, off the coast of southwest Spain, twenty-seven ships belonging to the British Navy, led by Vice-Admiral Horatio Nelson, traded blows with a combined fleet of French and Spanish vessels thirty-three strong, in a stage of the Napoleonic Wars now known as the Battle of Trafalgar. The British were victorious, comfortably so, and Napoléon Bonaparte's plans to invade were scuppered, but there were many deaths, including that of Nelson who died a hero. Two days before the battle, fully aware that he may not see her again, Nelson began writing to his mistress, Lady Emma Hamilton. The letter was discovered, unfinished, on his desk on HMS Victory, *following his death.*

THE LETTER

Victory Octr 19th 1805
Noon Cadiz ESE 16 Leagues

My Dearest beloved Emma the dear friend of my bosom the Signal has been made that the Enemys Combined fleet are coming out of Port. We have very little Wind so that I have no hopes of seeing them before tomorrow May the God of Battles crown my endeavours with success at all events I will take care that my name shall ever be most dear to you and Horatia both of whom I love as much as my own life, and as my last writing before the battle will be to you so I hope in God that I shall live to finish my letter after the Battle. May Heaven bless you prays your Nelson & Bronte.

Oct 20th, in the morning we were close to the mouth of the Streights but the Wind had not come far enough to the Westward to allow the Combined Fleets to Weather the shoals off Trafalgar but they were counted as far as forty Sail of Ships of War which I suppose to be 34 of the Line and six frigates, a Group of them was seen off the Lighthouse of Cadiz this Morng but it blows so very fresh & thick weather that I rather believe they will go into the Harbour before night. May God Almighty give us success over these fellows and enable us to get a Peace.

'AS MY LAST WRITING BEFORE THE BATTLE WILL BE TO YOU SO I HOPE IN GOD THAT I SHALL LIVE TO FINISH MY LETTER AFTER THE BATTLE.'

– Lord Horatio Nelson

LETTER 16
EXHAUSTED BUT EXHILARATED
June Wandrey to her sister, Betty
28 March 1945

Born in Wautoma, Wisconsin, in 1920, June Wandrey graduated from nursing school in Rochester, Minnesota, on 1 December 1940. Six days later, the Japanese attacked Pearl Harbor, thereby provoking the US to enter World War II. Wandrey enlisted with the United States Army Nurse Corps as soon as she could, and went on to serve as a combat nurse across North Africa and Europe until 1946, by which time she was First Lieutenant and had been awarded eight service stars for her efforts. In March 1945 she wrote home to her sister, Betty, and spoke of the incredible moment when Allied troops liberated Stalag XIIA, a former insane asylum in which hundreds of prisoners of war, some horrifically injured, had been held.

THE LETTER

3-28-45
Germany

Dearest Betty,

When I got off duty, I heard that our troops had liberated a POW hospital with hundreds of patients several miles from us, in a place called Heppenheim. Although it had started to rain and was getting dark and I was exhausted, I wanted to visit the prisoner-patients. Nobody wanted to risk hitchhiking with me, so dressed in my usual ill-fitting mannish garb, topped by my helmet and sloppy raincoat, with my pockets filled with my pitifully small supply of cigarettes and hard candy rations, I took off by myself through the mud . . . without permission.

Carefully slipping out of my tent, I disappeared in the blackness. After walking about a mile and a half, I was thoroughly soaked when I heard a jeep creeping along behind me in the blackout. I was walking in the middle of the road as the mines are only swept to the ditches. To keep from being hit I shouted "How about a lift?"

The jeep stopped. A very surprised Captain Engle, the lone occupant, from the 3rd Division was going to the hospital to assess and investigate conditions. He promised me a round-trip lift. He was fluent in German as he had been born here. We had casually met a month before at a party.

Two hundred and ninety of the prisoners were scruffy, starving, wounded Americans. The prison population included Russians, French, Italians, Slavs and Moroccans. Some of our men had been there for seven months. Their smaller wounds were covered with toilet paper, their brutal amputations were covered with rags. The men had torn their field jackets in shreds to bind the primitive dressings. Their bodies were covered with scratches, inflicted when they clawed at their body lice.

Breakfast was a piece of wormy, black bread about two by four inches – a loaf of bread a day for eight to ten men. Lunch was a small bowl of potato-peeling soup with sometimes a little rice in it. If they didn't finish it for lunch a little water was added to it, and that was their supper. They were shaved sometimes once a month, rarely oftener. Once a month they got a clean sheet. Blankets were never changed nor laundered. If they vomited in bed, it just stayed there with them. Our men who could walk cared for those who couldn't get out of bed.

In the push through the Ardennes last December

the Germans captured two American doctors, who were sent to this hospital to take care of eight hundred patients with less than minimal equipment. One of the doctors I had met back in Sicily. There were no nurses, just two German x-ray technicians.

Our soldiers were allowed to write one letter in their long imprisonment. They had never received any replies. Cigarettes were nonexistent. The Morroccans who could walk outside made cigarettes of dry weeds and wrapping paper and sold them to the GIs for exorbitant sums. The bed patients were covered with festering bed sores from lack of care. Morphine was the only medication available.

Our troops had by-passed this village, leaving behind one lone GI who had become separated from his company. From their window, some patients saw him crouching at the corner of their building, rifle in hand. They sneaked out, brought him in, and showed him their horrible conditions. Finally he slipped out, found his company, and returned with them to liberate the hospital.

As American rations poured in, the men cried. The corridors were stacked with cartons of inappropriate food for these starved men and their shrunken stomachs, but I guess that was all that we had to give at that time. All those that could eat, stuffed themselves so full of rations that most everyone became nauseated. The walkers would go outside and vomit and then gorge themselves and vomit again. It was just for the taste of the food going down, they didn't worry about the return trip.

When an American died, the Germans wouldn't touch him. They'd make the GIs who were able to walk carry him out and dispose of the body. If one of the men died before he could eat his ration of black bread and slop soup the remaining fellows would fight over it but end up by giving everyone a nibble.

You should have heard the joyous shrieks when the men saw me walk through those sad, louse-ridden wards. I went cot to cot. They had dozens of questions, everyone talked at once. Some talked to me until they were hoarse. Others just stared in disbelief, some touched my cheek, my hair, my hands. Still others touched my rough, wet fatigue sleeves like they were made of gold cloth and satin. Tears ran down our faces. Everyone wanted to share their recently acquired cigarette and C rations with me . . . or they'd say, "If you can just wait a minute, we'll make you some coffee." The lump in my throat nearly choked me. It was difficult being carefree and gay. But they wanted laughter, and female chatter . . . and I tried. Blarney comes in handy.

A priest in the village had a secret radio on which he'd listen to the American broadcasts. He'd relay any news to the American doctors who in turn would whisper progress-messages to the men at night, when they made their rounds.

Most people will never be privileged like I was tonight.

Exhausted but exhilarated,

June

LETTER 17
KEEP IT AND HONOR IT ALWAYS
Tom O'Sullivan to his son, Conor
16 September 1996

The Bosnian War began in April 1992, lasted more than three years, and was a conflict between the Republic of Bosnia and Herzegovina, Croatia, and Serbia and Montenegro that cost upwards of 100,000 people their lives and displaced more than a million. On 16 September 1996, nine months after a peace agreement was signed, Major Tom O'Sullivan was serving in Bosnia as operations officer of the 4th Battalion, 67th Armor, Camp Colt. As that day was also his son's seventh birthday, he wrote a letter.

THE LETTER

Dear Conor,

I am very sorry that I could not be home for your seventh birthday, but I will soon be finished with my time here in Bosnia and will return to be with you again. You know how much I love you, and that's what counts the most. I think that all I will think about on your birthday is how proud I am to be your dad and what a great kid you are.

I remember the day you were born and how happy I was. It was the happiest I have ever been in my life and I will never forget that day. You were very little and had white hair. I didn't let anyone else hold you much because I wanted to hold you all the time. That day was so special to me that I think it is right to have a celebration each year to remember it.

There aren't any stores here in Bosnia, so I couldn't buy you any toys or souvenirs for your birthday. What I am sending you is something very special, though. It is a flag. This flag represents America and makes me proud each time I see it. When people here in Bosnia see it on our uniforms, on our vehicles, or flying above our camps, they know that it represents freedom and, for them, peace after many years of war.

Sometimes, this flag is even more important to them than it is to people who live in America because some Americans don't know much about the sacrifices it represents or the peace it has brought to places like Bosnia.

This flag was flown on the flagpole over the headquarters of Task Force 4-67 Armor, Camp Colt, in the Posavina Corridor of northern Bosnia-Herzegovina, on 16 September 1996. It was flown in honor of you on your seventh birthday. Keep it and honor it always.

Love,

Dad

LETTER 18
PLEASE SPARE HER
Poppy, Lionel and Freda Hewlett and Lord Kitchener
11 August 1914

It was by no means just humans who were called up for service during World War I. In fact, over the course of the four-year conflict, more than sixteen million animals – including horses (for transport), dogs (for companionship and security), pigeons (to deliver messages), canaries (to detect gas) and cats (to catch rats in the trenches) – also went to war, a huge number made possible thanks to the inclusion of animals from private households, many across the UK. Unsurprisingly, not all citizens gave up their beloved pets without a fight. Two months after the war began, fearing the unthinkable, three distraught children from Wigan in England wrote to the Secretary of State for War, Field Marshal Herbert Kitchener, and begged him not to take their pony, a photo of which was included. To their astonishment, a reply soon arrived from Kitchener's private secretary, who had a message to pass on.

THE LETTERS

>   THE COTTAGE,
>   HAIGH,
>   WIGAN.

>   Aug: 11th 14

Dear good Lord Kitchener,
We are writing for our pony, which we are very afraid may be taken for your army. <u>Please spare her</u>. Daddy says she is going to be a mother early next year and is 17 years old. It would break our hearts to let her go. We have given 2 others and 3 of our family are now fighting for you in the Navy.

Mother and all will do anything for you but <u>do please</u> let us keep old Betty & send official word quickly before anyone comes.

Your troubled little Britishers,

P., L. and Freda Hewlett.

* * *

War Office,
Whitehall,
S. W.

Lord Kitchener asks me to say in reply to your letter of the 11th August, that if you will show the enclosed note to anyone who comes to ask about your pony, he thinks it will be left to you quite safely.

"F. M. Lord Kitchener has decided that no horses under 15 hands shall be requisitioned belonging to the British family P. L. & Freda Hewlett."

To our good Lord Kitchener,
You are indeed kind to allow us to keep our dear old Betty. We met every post and hardly dared to hope you, who have so much to do, had had time to read our request — so little to you — so much to us. Thank you ever and ever so much. We have your photo and will never forget your kindness and hope to do each and all 'our little' for you and all the brave men who are working for and fighting for dear old England and all of us.

Always and ever your grateful British servants,
Poppy, Lionel and Freda Hewlett and also Betty.
God save Lord Kitchener and the King.

LETTER 19
THE MOST EXTRAORDINARY SCENE
Captain Reginald John Armes to his wife
24 December 1914

On Christmas Eve of 1914, five months into World War I, thousands of British and German troops on the Western Front agreed to put down their weapons, rise from the trenches, and greet each other peacefully. For the next few days, close to 100,000 men, British and German, chatted, exchanged gifts, sang carols and played football. They also, most importantly, were able to bury their dead without fearing for their own safety. On the evening of 24 December, the first day of this amazing truce, Captain 'Jake' Armes of the 1st Battalion North Staffordshire Regiment wrote to his wife and described this incredible occurrence. Armes did return home to his family after the war and lived until 1948.

THE LETTER

24/12/14

I have just been through one of the most extraordinary scenes imaginable. To-night is Xmas Eve and I came up into the trenches this evening for my tour of duty in them. Firing was going on all the time and the enemy's machine guns were at it hard, firing at us. Then about seven the firing stopped.

I was in my dug-out reading a paper and the mail was being dished out. It was reported that the Germans had lighted their trenches up all along our front. We had been calling to one another for some time Xmas wishes and other things. I went out and they shouted "no shooting" and then somehow the scene became a peaceful one. All our men got out of their trenches and sat on the parapet, the Germans did the same, and they talked to one another in English and broken English. I got on top of the trench and talked German and asked them to sing a German Volkslied, which they did, then our men sang quite well and each side clapped and cheered the other.

I asked a German who sang a solo to sing one of Schumann's songs, so he sang "The Two

Grenadiers" splendidly. Our men were a good audience and really enjoyed his singing.

Then Pope and I walked across and held a conversation with the German Officer in command. One of his men introduced us properly, he asked my name and then presented me to his Officer. I gave the latter permission to bury some German dead who are lying in between us, and we agreed to have no shooting until 12 midnight to-morrow. We talked together, 10 or more Germans gathered round. I was almost in their lines within a yard or so. We saluted each other, he thanked me for permission to bury his dead, and we fixed up how many men were to do it, and that otherwise both sides must remain in their trenches.

Then we wished one another goodnight and a good night's rest, and a happy Xmas and parted with a salute. I got back to the trench. The Germans sang "Die Wacht Am Rhein", it sounded well. Then our men sang quite well "Christians Awake", it sounded so well, and with a good night we all got back into our trenches. It was a curious scene, a lovely moonlit night, the German trenches with small lights on them, and the men on both sides gathered in groups on the parapets.

At times we heard the guns in the distance and an occasional rifle shot. I can hear them now, but about us is absolute quiet. I allowed one or two men to go out and meet a German or two half way. They exchanged cigars, a smoke and talked. The Officer I spoke to hopes we shall do the same on New Year's Day, I said "yes, if I am here." I felt I must sit down and write the story of this Xmas Eve before I went to lie down. Of course no precautions are relaxed, but I think they mean to play the game. All the same, I think I shall be awake all night so as to be on the safe side. It is weird to think that to-morrow night we shall be at it hard again. If one gets through this show it will be a Xmas time to live in one's memory. The German who sang had a really fine voice.

Am just off for a walk round the trenches to see all is well. Good-night.

<u>Xmas Day</u>. We had an absolutely quiet night in front of us, though just to our right and left there was sniping going on. In my trenches and in those of the Enemy opposite to us were only nice big fires blazing, and occasional songs and conversation. This morning at the Reveille the Germans sent out parties to bury their dead. Our men went out to help, and then we all on both sides met in the middle, and in groups began to talk and exchange gifts of tobacco, etc. All this

morning we have been fraternising, singing songs. I have been within a yard in fact to their trenches, have spoken to and exchanged greetings with a Colonel, Staff Officers and several Company Officers. All were very nice and we fixed up that the men should not go near their opponents' trenches, but remain about midway between the lines. The whole thing is extraordinary. The men were all so natural and friendly. Several photos were taken, a group of German Officers, a German Officer and myself, and a group of British and German soldiers.

The Germans are Saxons, a good-looking lot, only wishing for peace in a manly way, and they seem in no way at their last gasp. I was astonished at the easy way in which our men and theirs got on with each other.

We have just knocked off for dinner, and have arranged to meet again afterwards until dusk when we go in again and have [illegible] until 9 p.m., when War begins again. I wonder who will start the shooting! They say "fire in the air and we will", and such things, but of course it will start and to-morrow we shall be at it hard killing one another. It is an extraordinary state of affairs which allows of a "Peace Day". I have never seen men so pleased to have a day off as both sides.

Their Opera Singer is going to give us a song or two to-night and perhaps I may give them one. Try and imagine two lines of trenches in peace, only 50 yards apart, the men of either side have never seen each other except perhaps a head now and again, and have never been outside in front of their trenches. Then suddenly one day men stream out and nest in friendly talk in the middle. One fellow, a married man, wanted so much a photo of Betty and Nancy in bed, which I had, and I gave him it as I had two: it seems he showed it all round, as several Germans told me afterwards about it. He gave me a photo of himself and family taken the other day which he had just got.

Well must finish now so as to get this off to-day. Have just finished dinner. Pork chop. Plum pudding. Mince pies. Ginger, and bottle of Wine and a cigar, and have drunk to all at home and especially to you, my darling one. Must go outside now to supervise the meetings of the men and the Germans.

Will try and write more in a day or two. Keep this letter carefully and send copies to all. I think they will be interested. It did feel funny walking over alone towards the enemy's trenches to meet someone half-way, and then to arrange a Xmas peace. It will be a thing to remember all one's life.

Kiss the babies and give them my love. Write me a long letter and tell me all the news. I hope the photos come out all right. Probably you will see them in some paper.
Yours,
(signed) JAKE.

LETTER 20
CORNWALLIS AND HIS ARMY ARE OURS
Alexander Hamilton to his wife, Elizabeth
October 1781

On 17 October 1781, on the battlefield at Yorktown, Virginia, an officer stood atop a trench and waved a white handkerchief on behalf of the British Army's commander, Charles Cornwallis, thereby signalling the end of the three-week-long Siege of Yorktown and, in effect, the American Revolutionary War of which it was the last major battle. The British surrender was forced in part by the actions of Alexander Hamilton, who nights before had led a double-headed attack that resulted in the capture of two British redoubts (temporary forts) and little room for Cornwallis to manoeuvre. Shortly after his strategy bore fruit, Hamilton wrote home to his wife with the news. Two days later, he wrote again.

THE LETTERS

[Yorktown, Virginia, October 16, 1781]

Two nights ago, my Eliza, my duty and my honor obliged me to take a step in which your happiness was too much risked. I commanded an attack upon one of the enemy's redoubts; we carried it in an instant, and with little loss. You will see the particulars in the Philadelphia papers. There will be, certainly, nothing more of this kind; all the rest will be by approach; and if there should be another occasion, it will not fall to my turn to execute it.

* * *

[Yorktown, Virginia, October 18, 1781]

Your letter of the 3d. of September my angel never reached me till to day. My uneasiness at not hearing from you is abated by the sweet prospect of soon taking you in my arms. Your father will tell you the news. Tomorrow Cornwallis and his army are ours. In two days after I shall in all probability set out for Albany, and I hope to embrace you in three weeks from this time. Conceive my love by your own feelings, how delightful this prospect is to me.

Only in your heart and in my own can any image be found of my happiness upon the occasion. I have no time to enlarge. Let the intilligence I give compensate for the shortness of my letter. Give my love to your Mama to Mrs. Carter to Peggy and to all the family.

Adieu My Charming beloved wife, I kiss you a thousand times, Adieu,

My love

A Hamilton

LETTER 21
WHY CAN'T WE HAVE A SOLDIER'S PAY?
James Henry Gooding to President Abraham Lincoln
28 September 1863

Born into slavery in North Carolina in August 1838, James Gooding was twenty-four years old when, in February 1863, he enlisted with the 54th Massachusetts Infantry Regiment – only the second regiment to consist of African-Americans – and began to fight in the American Civil War. Perhaps his most important contribution came in September when he wrote this letter to US President Abraham Lincoln and made clear, with great eloquence, his dissatisfaction with the salary disparity between white and black soldiers. His plea did not fall on deaf ears, and in June the following year, that gap was closed by a newly passed law granting equal pay to soldiers of all creeds. Sadly, Gooding would never know: he had been wounded in battle months earlier and taken prisoner. He died in a prison camp in July 1864.

THE LETTER

> Morris Island, S.C.
> September 28, 1863

Your Excellency, Abraham Lincoln:
Your Excellency will pardon the presumption of an humble individual like myself, in addressing you, but the earnest Solicitation of my Comrades in Arms besides the genuine interest felt by myself in the matter is my excuse, for placing before the Executive head of the Nation our Common Grievance: On the 6th of the last Month, the Paymaster of the Department informed us, that if we would decide to receive the sum of $10 (ten dollars) per month, he would come and pay us that sum, but that, on the sitting of Congress, the Regt. would, in his opinion, be allowed the other 3 (three). He did not give us any guarantee that this would be, as he hoped; certainly he had no authority for making any such guarantee, and we cannot suppose him acting in any way interested. Now the main question is, Are we Soldiers, or are we Labourers? We are fully armed, and equipped, have done all the various Duties pertaining to a Soldier's life, have conducted ourselves, to the complete satisfaction of General Officers, who were, if any,

prejudiced against us, but who now accord us all the encouragement and honors due us; have shared the perils, and Labour of Reducing the first stronghold that flaunted a Traitor Flag; and more, Mr. President. Today the Anglo-Saxon Mother, Wife, or Sister, are not alone, in tears for departed Sons, Husbands, and Brothers. The patient Trusting Descendants of Africs Clime, have dyed the ground with blood, in defense of the Union, and Democracy. Men too your Excellency, who know in a measure, the cruelties of the Iron heel of oppression, which in years gone by, the very Power, their blood is now being spilled to maintain, ever ground them to the dust. But When the war trumpet sounded o'er the land, when men knew not the Friend from the Traitor, the Black man laid his life at the Altar of the Nation, and he was refused. When the arms of the Union, were beaten, in the first year of the War, And the Executive called more food for its ravaging maw, again the black man begged, the privilege of Aiding his Country in her need, to be again refused And now, he is in the War: and how has he conducted himself? Let their dusky forms, rise up, out the mires of James Island, and give the answer. Let the rich mould around Wagners parapets be upturned, and there will be found an Eloquent answer. Obedient and patient, and Solid as a wall are they. All we lack, is a paler hue, and a better acquaintance with the Alphabet. Now Your Excellency, We have done a Soldiers duty. Why cant we have a Soldiers pay? You caution the Rebel Chieftain, that the United States, knows, no distinction in her Soldiers: She insists on having all her Soldiers, of whatever creed, or Color, to be treated, according to the usages of War. Now if the United States exacts uniformity of treatment of her Soldiers, from the Insurgents, would it not be well, and consistent, to set the example herself, by paying all her Soldiers alike? We of this Regt. were not enlisted under any "contraband" act. But we do not wish to be understood, as rating our Service, of more Value to the Government, than the service of the exslave, Their Service is undoubtedly worth much to the Nation, but Congress made express, provision touching their case, as slaves freed by military necessity, and assuming the Government, to be their temporary Guardian:- Not so with us – Freemen by birth, and consequently, having the advantage of thinking, and acting for ourselves, so far as the Laws would allow us. We do not consider ourselves fit subjects for the Contraband act. We appeal to You, Sir: as the Executive of the Nation, to have us Justly Dealt with. The Regt. do pray, that they be assured their service will be fairly appreciated, by paying them as American Soldiers, not as menial hierlings. Black men, You may well know, are poor, three dollars per month, for a year, will supply their needy Wives, and little ones, with fuel. If you, as chief Magistrate of the Nation, will assure us, of our whole pay. We are content, our Patriotism, our enthusiasm will have a new impetus, to exert our energy more and more to aid Our Country. Not that our hearts ever flagged, in Devotion, spite the evident apathy displayed in our behalf, but We feel as though, our Country spurned us, now we are sworn to serve her. Please give this a moments attention.

James Henry Gooding

> 'NOW YOUR EXCELLENCY, WE HAVE DONE A SOLDIERS DUTY. WHY CANT WE HAVE A SOLDIERS PAY?'
> — James Henry Gooding

LETTER 22
THIS IS QUITE TRUE
Evelyn Waugh to Laura Waugh
31 May 1942

Best known for his 1945 novel Brideshead Revisited, *English novelist Evelyn Waugh spent the five years preceding its publication in the military, first in the Royal Marines and then, thanks to a transfer in May 1942, the Royal Horse Guards, stationed at the time in southwest Scotland. This change of pace and scenery was much welcomed, not least as his wife, Laura, was at home many miles away, looking after their three children. She was also very pregnant with their fourth. On 31 May, a mere ten days before she gave birth to their daughter, Margaret, Evelyn put pen to paper and brightened her day considerably with a letter, perhaps the funniest he ever wrote, in which he told a tale involving a tree stump, some questionable mathematics and an overabundance of explosives.*

THE LETTER

31st May 1942

Darling
It was a great joy to get a letter from you. I
thought you had been swallowed up in some
Pixton plague.

Do you know Ellwoods address? I wrote to him
care Harper – no answer.

Miss Cowles leaves tonight. Everyone except me
will be sorry. I have had to arrange all her
movements and it has been a great deal of trouble.
She is a cheerful, unprincipled young woman. She
wants to be made Colonel in chief of the
commando so I have suggested Princess Margaret
Rose instead. Bob eats out of my hand at the
moment.

So No. 3 Cmdo were very anxious to be chums
with Lord Glasgow so they offered to blow up an
old tree stump for him and he was very grateful
and he said don't spoil the plantation of young
trees near it because that is the apple of my eye
and they said no of course not we can blow a tree
down so that it falls on a sixpence and Lord
Glasgow said goodness you are clever and he asked
them all to luncheon for the great explosion. So

Col. Durnford-Slater D.S.O. said to his subaltern, have you put enough explosive in the tree. Yes, sir, 75 lbs. Is that enough? Yes sir I worked it out by mathematics it is exactly right. Well better put a bit more. Very good sir.

And when Col. D. Slater D.S.O. had had his port he sent for the subaltern and said subaltern better put a bit more explosive in that tree. I don't want to disappoint Lord Glasgow. Very good sir.

Then they all went out to see the explosion and Col. D.S. D.S.O. said you will see that tree fall flat at just that angle where it will hurt no young trees and Lord Glasgow said goodness you are clever.

So soon they lit the fuse and waited for the explosion and presently the tree, instead of falling quietly sideways, rose 50 feet into the air taking with it ½ acre of soil and the whole of the young plantation.

And the subaltern said Sir I made a mistake, it should have been 7½ lbs not 75.

Lord Glasgow was so upset he walked in dead silence back to his castle and when they came to the turn of the drive in sight of his castle what should they find but that every pane of glass in the building was broken.

So Lord Glasgow gave a little cry & ran to hide his emotion in the lavatory and there when he pulled the plug the entire ceiling, loosened by the explosion, fell on his head.

This is quite true.

E

LETTER 23
THE ZULUS WERE ON US AT ONCE
Lieutenant Henry Curling to his mother
2 February 1879

The Anglo-Zulu War was an ugly testament to the British Empire's colonial days: a brutal series of encounters that took place in the South African kingdom of Zulu, after an invasion by the British. In July 1879, following six months of fighting and thousands of deaths, the British Empire defeated the Zulu army, but not until after the latter had inflicted considerable losses on the British. The first major conflict, on 22 January 1879, was the Battle of Isandlwana, during which almost 20,000 Zulu warriors overwhelmed the invading forces and killed more than 1,300 soldiers, thus inflicting a defeat so heavy that just one frontline officer survived: Lieutenant Henry Curling of the Royal Artillery. Soon after his lucky escape, Curling wrote home to his mother and described the battle in great detail. His letter, one of few first-hand accounts from the front, was later reprinted in The Standard. *Curling retired from the British Army in 1902 and settled in Ramsgate where he died in 1910.*

THE LETTER

>Feb 2nd
>Natal

My dear Mama,
Now things have quieted down again a little, I can tell you more about what has happened. I trust you had no false report: I saw the first man who went into Pietermaritzburg with the news and I hope you may have had no anxiety.

On the morning of the fight, the main body left at 3.30 in the morning, a little before daylight, leaving us with two guns and about 70 men. About 7.30 we were turned out as about 1000 Zulus were seen in some hills about 2 miles from the camp. We did not think anything of it and I was congratulating myself on having an independent command. I had out with my guns only 20 men, the remainder 50 in number stayed in the camp. We remained formed up in front of the camp (it was about 1/2 mile long) until 11 o'clock, when the enemy disappeared behind some hills on our left, we returned to camp. We none of us had the least idea that the Zulus contemplated attacking the camp and, having in the last war often seen equally large bodies of the enemy, never dreamed they would come on. Besides, we had about 600 troops (regulars), two guns, about 100 other white men and at least 1000 armed natives.

About 12, as the men were getting their dinner, the alarm was again given and we turned out at once. Maj. Smith came back from the General's force at this time and took command. This of course relieved me of all responsibility as to the movement of the guns. We, being mounted, moved off before the infantry and took up a position to the left front of the camp where we were able to throw shells into a huge mass of the enemy that remained almost stationary. The 24th Regt. came up and formed in skirmishing order on both our flanks. The Zulus soon split up into a large mass of skirmishers that extended as far round the camp as we would see.

We could form no idea of numbers but the hills were black with them. They advanced steadily in the face of the infantry and our guns but I believe the whole of the natives who defended the rear of the camp soon bolted and left only our side of the camp defended. Very soon bullets began to whistle about our heads and the men began to fall.

The Zulus still continued to advance and we began to fire case but the order was given to retire after firing a round or two.

At this time, out of my small detachment, one man had been killed, shot through the head, another wounded, shot through the side and another through the wrist. Maj. Smith was also shot through the arm but was able to do his duty. Of course, no wounded man was attended to, there was no time or men to spare. When we got the order to retire, we limbered up at once but were hardly in time as the Zulus were on us at once and one man was killed (stabbed) as he was mounting in a seat on the gun carriage. Most of the gunners were on foot as there was not time to mount them on the guns.

We trotted off to the camp thinking to take up another position but found it was in possession of the enemy who were killing the men as they ran out of their tents. We went right through them and out the other side, losing nearly all our gunners in doing so and one of the two sergeants. The road to Rorke's Drift that we hoped to retreat by was full of the enemy so, no way being open, we followed a crowd of natives and camp followers who were running down a ravine. The Zulus were all among them, stabbing men as they ran.

The ravine got steeper and steeper and finally the guns stuck and could get no further. In a moment the Zulus closed in and the drivers, who now alone remained, were pulled off their horses and killed. I did not see Maj. Smith at this moment but was with him a minute before.

The guns could not be spiked, there was no time to think of anything and we hoped to save the guns up to the last moment.

As soon as the guns were taken, I galloped off and made off with the crowd. How any of us escaped, I don't know; the Zulus were all around us and I saw men falling all round. We rode for about 5 miles, hotly pursued by the Zulus, when we came to a cliff overhanging the river. We had to climb down the face of the cliff and not more than half those who started from the top got to the bottom. Many fell right down, among other, Maj. Smith and the Zulus caught us here and shot us as we climbed down. I got down safety and came to the river which was very deep and swift. Numbers were swept away as they tried to cross and others shot from above.

My horse, fortunately, swam straight across, though I had three or four men hanging on his tail, stirrup leathers, etc. After crossing the river, we were in comparative safety, though many were killed afterwards who were on foot and unable to keep up. It seems to me like a dream, I cannot realise it at all. The whole affair did not last an hour from beginning to end. Many got away from the camp but were killed in the retreat. No officers or men of the 24th Regt. could escape: they were all on foot and on the other side of the camp. I saw two of them, who were not with their men, near the river but their bodies were found afterwards on our side of the river.

Of the 50 men we left in camp, 8 managed to escape on spare horses we had left in camp. One sergeant only, of my detachment, got away. Altogether, we lost 62 men and 24 horses, just half the battery.

Those who have escaped have not a rag left as they came away in their shirt sleeves. We always sleep at night in the fort or laager, as it is called, and in the open air. It is very unpleasant as it rains nearly every night and is very cold.

We none of us have more than one blanket each, so you can see we are having a rough time. The first few days I was utterly done up but have pulled round all right now.

What is going to happen, no one knows. We have made a strong entrenchment and are pretty safe even should we be attacked. The only thing we are afraid of is sickness. There are 50 sick and wounded already who are all jammed up at night in the fort. The smell is terrible, 800 men cooped up in so small a place. Food, fortunately, is plentiful and we have at least a three months supply. All spys taken now are shot: we have disposed of three or four already.

Formerly, they were allowed anywhere and our disaster is to a great extent due to their accurate information of the General's movements. What excitement this will cause in England and what indignation.

The troops, of course, were badly placed and the arrangements for defending the camp indifferent but there should have been enough troops and the risk of leaving a small force to be attacked by 10 to 15 times its number should not have been allowed. As you have heard, there were no wounded, all the wounded were killed in a most horrible way. I saw several wounded men during the retreat, all crying out for help, as they knew the terrible fate in store for them. Smith-Dorrien, a young fellow in the 95 Regt., I saw dismount and try to help one. His horse was killed in a minute by a shot and he had to run for his life only escaping by a miracle. You will see all sorts of accounts in the papers and no end of lies. Most of those who escaped were volunteers and native contingent officers who tell any number of lies. We hear the General has telegraphed for 6 Regiments and a cavalry Brigade. Even with these troops, it will take a long time to finish the war. It takes months to accustom troops to the country and in fact they are quite unfit for fighting in the Field as they require such enormous baggage trains. The colonial troops move without anything and always sleep in the open. We shall get no assistance from natives now as they do not believe in us anymore.

Your letters still arrive pretty regularly and are a great treat. I am very sorry to hear about Emmy but trust it is only a mild attack. It is unfortunate, as it will delay your journey very much.

I am very glad Papa continues pretty well. It will be rather a risk crossing the channel and travelling through France if the weather continues so severe. I think I must be promoted by now: I do hope I may get a good fall. It will be depressing indeed if I get out of this safely to be sent to some out of the way part of the world.

All those who escaped have sent in reports, by order, which will probably be published, so you will hear eventually the truth about this sad disaster. The General, poor fellow, seemed quite off his head and so nothing is being done, nor it would seem, has he recovered himself yet.

Give my love to all at home and believe me,
Your most affect Son
H T Curling

LETTER 24
THESE THINGS AREN'T TRIVIAL TO ME
Captain Rodney R. Chastant to his parents
19 October 1967

On 19 October 1967, newly appointed Captain Rodney R. Chastant proudly wrote this letter home from Vietnam with news of his recent promotion. The next year, in September 1968, he wrote another letter explaining that he was extending his tour of duty rather than returning home, because 'my experience is invaluable. This job requires a man of conscience.' Tragically, he was killed in action a month later.

THE LETTER

> Captain Rodney R. Chastant,
> 1st Marine Air Wing Vietnam,
> 19 October 67

Mom and Dad

Your oldest son is now a captain in the United States Marine Corps. I was promoted yesterday. Of all the men selected for captain, 1,640 men, only about 50 men have been promoted to date. I was one of the 50, to my surprise and pleasure. My effective date of rank is 1 July 1967, which means I have technically been a captain for 3½ months. I am thus due back pay for 3½ months. With this promotion, my annual income is $9,000 a year. I'm single, 24 years old, college-education, a captain in the Marine Corps, and I have $11,000 worth of securities. This is not a bad start in life, is it?

As I understand, Dad, you were married about this point in life. There was a war going on then too. I really know very little about those years in my parents' lives. Sometime you will have to tell me about them — what you were doing, what you were thinking, what you were planning, what you were hoping.

Mom, I appreciate all your letters. I appreciate your concern that some of the things you write about are trivial, but they aren't trivial to me. I'm eager to read anything about what you are doing or the family is doing. You can't understand the importance these "trivial" events take on out here. It helps keep me civilized. For a while, as I read your letters, I am a normal person. I'm not killing people, or worried about being killed. While I read your letters, I'm not carrying guns and grenades. Instead I am going ice skating with David or walking through a department store to exchange a lamp shade. It is great to know your family's safe, living in a secure country; a country made secure by thousands upon thousands of men who have died for that country.

In the Philippines I took a bus ride along the infamous route of the death march in Bataan. I passed graveyards that were marked with row after row after row of plain white crosses. Thousands upon thousands. These were Americarn graves — American graves in the Philippines. And I thought about the American graves in Okinawa, Korea, France, England, North Africa, around the world. And I was proud to be an American, proud to be a Marine, proud to be fighting in Asia. I have a commitment to the men who have gone before me, American men who made the sacrifices that were required to make the world safe for ice skating, department stores and lamp shades.

No, Mom, these things aren't trivial to me. They are vitally important to me. Those are the truly important things, not what I'm doing. I hope you will continue to write about those "trivial" things because that is what I enjoy learning about the most.

Your son,
Rod

LETTER 25
MY DEAR FAMILY, PLEASE FORGIVE ME
Alaa abd al-Akeedi to his family
2016

Ever since a US-led coalition of troops invaded Iraq in 2003 'to disarm [the country] of weapons of mass destruction, to end Saddam Hussein's support for terrorism, and to free the Iraqi people', the region has been the scene of unending violence and hundreds of thousands of deaths. In January 2014, eleven years after it all began and with those invading forces long gone, a civil war broke out between Iraqi forces and the terrorist organisation known as the Islamic State, who quickly took control of a number of cities. Much of their success can be traced to youngsters like sixteen-year-old Alaa abd al-Akeedi, who was recruited by the Islamic State when he was fifteen and trained to kill by suicide attack. His farewell letter, and those of dozens of other teenage jihadists, was found in an Islamic State training compound in the city of Mosul following its liberation in 2016.

THE LETTER

My dear family, please forgive me. Don't be sad and don't wear the black clothes of mourning. I asked to get married and you did not marry me off. So, by God, I will marry the 72 virgins in paradise.

LETTER 26
FOR THE SAKE OF HUMANITY
Mohandas Gandhi to Adolf Hitler
23 July 1939

In July of 1939, two months before the German invasion of Poland that prompted World War II, Mohandas Gandhi, leader of the Indian independence movement, penned a letter to Adolf Hitler and pleaded for peace 'for the sake of humanity'. A year later, with the world in turmoil, he wrote again with more force. Unbeknownst to Gandhi, neither of his letters reached the leader of Nazi Germany; instead, they were intercepted by the British Raj. Gandhi was also unaware that in late 1937, in a meeting with government envoy Lord Edward Halifax, Hitler had advised the British to 'Shoot Gandhi, and if this doesn't suffice to reduce [the Indian National Congress] to submission, shoot a dozen leading members of the Congress, and if that doesn't suffice shoot 200, and so on, as you make it clear that you mean business.'

THE LETTER

>As at Wardha
>C.P.
>23.7.'39.

Dear friend,

Friends have been urging me to write to you for the sake of humanity. But I have resisted their request, because of the feeling that any letter from me would be an impertinence. Something tells me that I must not calculate and that I must make my appeal for whatever it may be worth.

It is quite clear that you are today the one person in the world who can prevent a war which may reduce humanity to the savage state. Must you pay that price for an object however worthy it may appear to you to be? Will you listen to the appeal of one who has deliberately shunned the method of war not without considerable success? Any way I anticipate your forgiveness, if I have erred in writing to you.

I remain,
Your sincere friend
M.K. Gandhi

As at Wardha,
December 24, 1940

Dear friend,

That I address you as a friend is no formality. I own no foes. My business in life has been for the past 33 years to enlist the friendship of the whole of humanity by befriending mankind, irrespective of race, colour or creed.

I hope you will have the time and desire to know how a good portion of humanity who have view living under the influence of that doctrine of universal friendship view your action. We have no doubt about your bravery or devotion to your fatherland, nor do we believe that you are the monster described by your opponents. But your own writings and pronouncements and those of your friends and admirers leave no room for doubt that many of your acts are monstrous and unbecoming of human dignity, especially in the estimation of men like me who believe in universal friendliness. Such are your humiliation of Czechoslovakia, the rape of Poland and the swallowing of Denmark. I am aware that your view of life regards such spoliations as virtuous acts. But we have been taught from childhood to regard them as acts degrading humanity. Hence we cannot possibly wish success to your arms.

But ours is a unique position. We resist British Imperialism no less than Nazism. If there is a difference, it is in degree. One-fifth of the human race has been brought under the British heel by means that will not bear scrutiny. Our resistance to it does not mean harm to the British people. We seek to convert them, not to defeat them on the battle-field. Ours is an unarmed revolt against the British rule. But whether we convert them or not, we are determined to make their rule impossible by non-violent non-co-operation. It is a method in its nature indefensible. It is based on the knowledge that no spoliator can compass his end without a certain degree of co-operation, willing or compulsory, of the victim. Our rulers may have our land and bodies but not our souls. They can have the former only by complete destruction of every Indian—man, woman and child. That all may not rise to that degree of heroism and that a fair amount of frightfulness can bend the back of revolt is true but the argument would be beside the point. For, if a fair number of men and women be found in India who would be prepared without any ill will against the spoliators to lay down their lives rather than bend the knee to them, they would have shown the way to freedom from the tyranny of violence. I ask you to believe me when I say that you will find an unexpected number of such men and women in India. They have been having that training for the past 20 years.

We have been trying for the past half a century to throw off the British rule. The movement of independence has been never so strong as now. The most powerful political organization, I mean the Indian National Congress, is trying to achieve this end. We have attained a very fair measure of success through non-violent effort. We were groping for the right means to combat the most organized violence in the world which the British power represents. You have challenged it. It remains to be seen which is the better organized, the German or the British. We know what the British heel means for us and the non-European races of the world. But we would never wish to end the British rule with German aid. We have found in non-violence a force which, if organized, can without doubt match itself against a combination of all the most violent forces in the world. In non-violent technique, as I have said, there is no such thing as defeat. It is all 'do or die' without killing or hurting. It can be used practically without money and obviously without the aid of science of destruction which you have brought to such perfection. It is a marvel to me that you do not see that it is nobody's monopoly. If not the British, some other power will certainly improve upon your method and beat you with your own weapon. You are leaving no legacy to your people of which they would feel proud. They cannot take pride in a recital of cruel deed, however skilfully planned. I, therefore, appeal to you in the name of humanity to stop the war. You will lose nothing by referring all the matters of dispute between you and Great Britain to an international tribunal of your joint choice. If you attain success in the war, it will not prove that you were in the right. It will only prove that your power of destruction was greater. Whereas an award by an impartial tribunal will show as far as it is humanly possible which party was in the right.

You know that not long ago I made an appeal to every Briton to accept my method of non-violent resistance. I did it because the British know me as a friend though a rebel. I am a stranger to you and your people. I have not the courage to make you the appeal I made to every Briton. Not that it would not apply to you with the same force as to the British. But my present proposal is much simple because much more practical and familiar.

During this season when the hearts of the

peoples of Europe yearn for peace, we have suspended even our own peaceful struggle. Is it too much to ask you to make an effort for peace during a time which may mean nothing to you personally but which must mean much to the millions of Europeans whose dumb cry for peace I hear, for my ears are attended to hearing the dumb millions? I had intended to address a joint appeal to you and Signor Mussolini, whom I had the privilege of meeting when I was in Rome during my visit to England as a delegate to the Round Table Conference. I hope that he will take this as addressed to him also with the necessary changes.

I am,

Your sincere friend,

M. K. GANDHI

LETTER 27
THE SONS OF HAM
M.W. Saddler to the *Freeman* newspaper
30 July 1898

On 1 July 1898 Spanish and Cuban soldiers attempted to hold Santiago de Cuba and fight off American troops in what was the Battle of El Caney. Their efforts were fruitless, and the US, led by Brigadier General Henry Ware Lawton, were ultimately victorious. Weeks later, having seen no report of the battle in the publication, a soldier who had helped to defeat the Spanish, named M.W. Saddler, wrote to the Freeman *newspaper to proudly boast of his regiment's achievements.*

THE LETTER

July 30, 1898

Dear Sir

I wish to call attention to the heroic part the Twenty-fifth United States Infantry played in compelling the surrender of Santiago. We have no reporter in the division and it appears that we are coming up unrepresented.

On the morning of July 1, our regiment, having slept part of the night with stones for pillows and heads resting on hands, arose at the dawn of day, without a morsel to eat, formed line, and after a half day of hard marching, succeeded in reaching the bloody battleground at El Caney. We were in the last brigade of our division. As we were marching up we met regiments of our comrades in white retreating from the Spanish stronghold. As we pressed forward all the reply that came from the retiring soldiers was: "There is no use to advance further. The Spaniards are intrenched and in block houses. You are running to sudden death." But without a falter did our brave men continue to press to the front.

In a few minutes the desired position was reached. The first battalion of the Twenty-fifth

Infantry, composed of companies C, D, G and H were ordered to form the firing line, in preference to other regiments, though the commanders were seniors to ours. But no sooner was the command given than the execution began. A thousand yards distance to the north lay the enemy, 2000 strong in intrenchments hewn out of solid stone. On each end of the breastwork were stone block houses. Our regiment numbered 507 men all told. We advanced about 200 yards under cover of jungles and ravines. Then came the trying moments. The clear battlefield was reached. The enemy began showering down on us volleys from their strong fortifications and numberless sharpshooters hid away in palm trees and other places . . .

Our men began to fall, many of them never to rise again, but so steady was the advance and so effective was our fire that the Spaniards became unnerved and began over-shooting us. When they saw we were "colored soldiers" they knew their doom was sealed. They were afraid to put their heads above the brink of their intrenchments for every time a head was raised there was one Spaniard less.

The advance was continued until we were within about 150 yards of the intrenchments; then came the solemn command, "Charge." Every man was up and rushing forward at headlong speed over the barbed wire and into the intrenchments, and the Twenty-fifth carried the much coveted position.

So great was the loss of officers that Company C had to be commanded by its First Sergeant S. W. Taliaferro, the gallant aspirant for the commission from the ranks . . . The Company's commander was wounded early in the action by the explosion of a bombshell.

Thus our people can now see that the coolness and bravery that characterized our fathers in the 60's have been handed down to their sons of the 90's. If any one doubts the fitness of a colored soldier for active field service, when the cry of musketry, the booming of cannon and bursting of shells, seem to make the earth tremble, ask the regimental Commanders of the Twenty-fourth and Twenty-fifth infantries and Ninth and Tenth Cavalry. Ask Generals Lawton, Kent and Wheeler, of whose divisions these regiments formed a part.

The Spaniards call us "Negretter Solados" and say there is no use shooting at us, for steel and powder will not stop us. We only hope our brethren will come over and help us to show to the world that true patriotism is in the minds of the sons of Ham. All we need is leaders of our own race to make war records, so that their names may go down in history as a reward for the price of our precious blood.

M.W. Saddler
First Sergeant, Co.D
25th Inf.

LETTER 28
IT IS ALL GOING TO HELL
Martha Gellhorn to Eleanor Roosevelt
March 1938

During an illustrious career that spanned more than half a century, celebrated war correspondent Martha Gellhorn travelled the world to report on numerous conflicts, from the Spanish Civil War through to the Cold War, and touching on most wars in-between. In December 1936, in a bar named Sloppy Joe's in Key West, Florida, she met and fell for fellow writer Ernest Hemingway, and within months they had decided to travel to Spain together, where she would be reporting on Spain's civil war for Collier's *magazine. In March 1938, as they sailed back to Spain following a break in Miami, Gellhorn wrote to her friend, First Lady Eleanor Roosevelt, and spoke of her dismay at the situation in Europe – and correctly predicted another world war which was only a year away.*

THE LETTER

March 1938
RMS *Queen Mary*

Dearest Mrs R —

I wanted to see you, and hoped all the time you'd be in Washington and that I'd get there. Then you were out west, and anyhow I decided on Sunday night in St Louis to sail, & sailed Wednesday morning and there was no time for anything.

The news from Spain has been terrible, too terrible, and I felt I had to get back. It is all going to hell . . . I want to be there, somehow sticking with the people who fight against Fascism. If there are survivors, we can then all go to Czechoslovakia. A fine life. It makes me helpless and crazy with anger to watch the next Great War hurtling towards us, and I think the 3 democracies (ours too, as guilty as the others) have since 1918 consistently muffled their role in history. Lately the behaviour of the English govt surpasses anything one could imagine for criminal, hypocritical incompetence, but am not dazzled either by us or France. It will work out the same way: the young men will die, the best ones will die first, and the old powerful men will survive to mishandle the peace. Everything in life I care about is nonsense in case of war. And all the people I love will finish up dead, before they can have done their work. I believe the people — in their ignorance, fear, supineness — are also responsible: but the original fault is not theirs. They control nothing: they react badly to misinformation & misdirection & later they can wipe out their mistake with their lives.

I don't believe that anything any of us does now is useful. We just have to do it. Articles & speeches hoping someone will hear & understand. And if they do, then what. The whole world is accepting destruction from the author of 'Mein Kampf', a man who cannot think straight for half a page.

I wish I could see you. But you wouldn't like me much. I have gone angry to the bone, and hating what I see, and knowing how it is in Spain, I can see it so clearly everywhere else. I think now maybe the only place at all is in the front lines, where you don't have to think, and can simply (and uselessly) put your body up against what you hate. Not that this does any good either . . . The war in Spain was one kind of war, the next world war will be the stupidest,

lyingest, cruellest sell-out in our time. Forgive this letter: I can't write any other kind,
   love
   Marty

LETTER 29
I HAVE DONE MY DUTY
John Duesbery to his mother
September 1916

On 1 July 1916 British and French soldiers advanced on German troops in northern France, thus beginning the Battle of the Somme, a particularly devastating four-and-a-half-month period of World War I during which three million soldiers fought for their country, hundreds of thousands of whom died. Almost 20,000 British soldiers were killed on the first day alone. John Duesbery was a twenty-five-year-old corporal from East Yorkshire serving with the 2nd Battalion, the Sherwood Foresters infantry regiment, and on the morning of 13 September 1916, he and his fellow soldiers were tasked with attacking a network of German-held trenches known as the Ginchy Quadrilateral. Duesbery was shot multiple times. As he lay dying, he wrote a letter to his mother. She received it many agonising months later, along with the rest of his belongings.

THE LETTER

Dear Mother

I am writing these few lines severely wounded. We have done well our Batt. advanced about 3 quarters of a mile. I am laid in a shell hole with 2 wounds in my hip and through my back. I cannot move or crawl. I have been here for 24 hours and never seen a living soul. I hope you will receive these few lines as I don't expect anyone will come to take me away, but you know I have done my duty out here now for 1 year and 8 months and you will always have the consolation that I died quite happy doing my duty.

Must give my best of love to all the cousins who have been so kind to me since I have been out here and the Best of love to Arthur and Harry and all at Swinefleet. xxx

LETTER 30
SLEEP WELL MY LOVE
Brian Keith to Dave
Date unknown

In June 1940, little under a year after World War II began, Italy joined forces with Nazi Germany, a development which resulted in the war spreading to North Africa until the Allies' victory in May 1943. Five months later, still stationed in North Africa, two soldiers met, fell in love, and imagined one day returning home together. Sadly, that never happened, as only Brian made the journey. He penned this love letter long after leaving the war, in memory of the first time he heard his lover's voice; it was reprinted in the September 1961 edition of One magazine, a groundbreaking pro-gay publication first published in 1953.

THE LETTER

Dear Dave,

This is in memory of an anniversary — the anniversary of October 27th, 1943, when I first heard you singing in North Africa. That song brings memories of the happiest times I've ever known. Memories of a GI show troop — curtains made from barrage balloons — spotlights made from cocoa cans — rehearsals that ran late into the evenings — and a handsome boy with a wonderful tenor voice. Opening night at a theatre in Canastel — perhaps a bit too much muscatel, and someone who understood. Exciting days playing in the beautiful and stately Municipal Opera House in Oran — a misunderstanding — an understanding in the wings just before opening chorus.

Drinks at "Coq d'or" — dinner at the "Auberge" — a ring and promise given. The show 1st Armoured — muscatel, scotch, wine — someone who had to be carried from the truck and put to bed in his tent. A night of pouring rain and two very soaked GIs beneath a solitary tree on an African plain. A borrowed French convertible — a warm sulphur spring, the cool Mediterranean, and a picnic of "rations" and hot cokes. Two lieutenants who were smart enough to know the score, but not smart enough to realize that we wanted to be alone. A screwball piano player — competition — miserable days and lonely nights. The cold, windy night we crawled through the window of a GI theatre and fell asleep on a cot backstage, locked in each other's arms — the shock when we awoke and realized that miraculously we hadn't been discovered. A fast drive to a cliff above the sea — pictures taken, and a stop amid the purple grapes and cool leaves of a vineyard.

The happiness when told we were going home — and the misery when we learned that we would not be going together. Fond goodbyes on a secluded beach beneath the star-studded velvet of an African night, and the tears that would not be stopped as I stood atop the sea-wall and watched your convoy disappear over the horizon.

We vowed we'd be together again "back home," but fate knew better — you never got there. And so, Dave, I hope that where ever you are these memories are as precious to you as they are to me.

Goodnight, sleep well my love.

Brian Keith

PERMISSION CREDITS

Every effort has been made to trace copyright holders and obtain their permission for the use of copyright material. The publisher apologises for any errors or omissions and would be grateful if notified of any corrections that should be incorporated in future reprints or editions of this book.

LETTER 1 Copyright © 2012, The Kurt Vonnegut Jr. Trust, used by permission of The Wylie Agency (UK) Limited. / From *Kurt Vonnegut: Letters* by Kurt Vonnegut, edited by Dan Wakefield Published by Vintage Classics Reprinted by permission of The Random House Group Limited. © 2013 / 'Letter: November 28, 1967' from *Kurt Vonnegut: Letters* by Kurt Vonnegut, edited by Dan Wakefield, copyright © 2012 by The Kurt Vonnegut, Jr. Trust. Used by permission of Delacorte Press, an imprint of Random House, a division of Penguin Random House LLC. All rights reserved.

LETTER 4 Frederic Krome, 'The Wartime Letters of Rabbi Morris Frank, 1944–1945,' *American Jewish Archives Journal* LIV, no. 2 (2002): 71–87. Original letters are held at The Jacob Rader Marcus Center of the American Jewish Archives (AJA), Cincinnati, OH, SC-15430.

LETTER 8 'Letter by Eleanor Wimbish' from *Dear America: Letters Home From Vietnam*, edited by Bernard Edelman. Copyright © 1985 by The Vietnam Veterans Memorial Commission. Used by permission of W. W. Norton & Company, Inc.

LETTER 13 Canute Frankson letter reproduced by kind permission of Abraham Lincoln Brigade Archives.

LETTER 16 Reprinted by kind permission of Gail Mann, Elmore Publishing.

LETTER 17 Tom O'Sullivan letter from *War Letters: Extraordinary Correspondence from American Wars* (New York: Scribner, 2001) edited by Andrew Carroll. Reprinted with permission.

LETTER 19 Reprinted by kind permission of Staffordshire Regiment Museum.

LETTER 22 Letter – May 31st 1942 by Evelyn Waugh. Copyright © 1942, The Estate of Laura Waugh, used by permission of The Wylie Agency (UK) Limited.

LETTER 24 'Letter by Rodney Chastant 19 October 1967', from *Dear America: Letters Home From Vietnam*, edited by Bernard Edelman. Copyright © 1985 by The Vietnam Veterans Memorial Commission. Used by permission of W. W. Norton & Company, Inc.

LETTER 28 By kind permission of Dr Alexander Matthews, literary executor for the Martha Gellhorn estate.

ACKNOWLEDGEMENTS

It requires a dedicated team of incredibly patient people to bring the Letters of Note books to life, and this page serves as a heartfelt thank you to every single one of them, beginning with my wife, Karina – not just for kickstarting my obsession with letters all those years ago, but for working with me as Permissions Editor, a vital and complex role. Special mention, also, to my excellent editor at Canongate Books, Hannah Knowles, who has somehow managed to stay focused despite the problems I have continued to throw her way.

Equally sincere thanks to all of the following: the one and only Jamie Byng, whose vision and enthusiasm for this series has proven invaluable; all at Canongate Books, including but not limited to Rafi Romaya, Kate Gibb, Vicki Rutherford and Leila Cruickshank; my dear family at Letters Live: Jamie, Adam Ackland, Benedict Cumberbatch, Aimie Sullivan, Amelia Richards and Nick Allott; my agent, Caroline Michel, and everyone else at Peters, Fraser & Dunlop; the many illustrators who have worked on the beautiful covers in this series; the talented performers who have lent their stunning voices not just to Letters Live, but also to the Letters of Note audiobooks; Patti Pirooz; every single archivist and librarian in the world; everyone at Unbound; the team at the Wylie Agency for their assistance and understanding; my foreign publishers for their continued support; and, crucially, my family, for putting up with me during this process.

Finally, and most importantly, thank you to all of the letter writers whose words feature in these books.